TREASURES FROM THE ARCHIVE

C. G. JUNG INSTITUTE ZÜRICH-KÜSNACHT

IMAGES CREATED BY PATIENTS IN ANALYSIS

1917 - 1955

Contact the Editor and Publisher, Dyane Sherwood, 280 Elm Street, Oberlin, OH 44074-1504, US.
Website: https://analyticalpsychologypress.com

This book was originally published in German in 2018 by Patmos Printing Group, www.patmos.com. This first English Edition is published by permission of Patmos Printing Group.

Translation from the German: Camilla Nielsen and Sibylle Pot d'Or
Design: Dyane Sherwood
Printed in the United Kingdom
Hard Cover Edition ISBN 978-1-958263-06-8
Library of Congress Control Number LCCN 2023931750

TREASURES FROM THE ARCHIVE

C.G. JUNG INSTITUTE ZÜRICH-KÜSNACHT

IMAGES CREATED BY PATIENTS IN ANALYSIS

1917 - 1955

EDITED BY RUTH AMMANN,

VERENA KAST, AND INGRID RIEDEL

ANALYTICAL PSYCHOLOGY PRESS

The publication of this book was supported by an anonymous donor

in honor of

Ruth Ammann

Contents

Catalogues: Thematic Selections from the Archive

Pictures are identified by their catalogue numbers in the Picture Archive of the C.G. Jung Institute Zürich-Küsnacht.

Preface

THE C.G. JUNG INSTITUTE Zürich, founded on April 24, 1948, celebrated its seventieth anniversary in 2018. On that occasion we decided to present something truly special which had not been previously accessible to the public, namely, works by patients from the Picture Archive of the Institute.

Starting in 1917, C.G. Jung encouraged his patients to draw or paint their dreams and fantasies. The imaginative act, the elaboration of images, the understanding of pictures as symbols, as well as the therapeutic effect of working with imagery, the use of symbolic design to eliminate splits in the psyche – all of this constitutes the very core of Jungian therapy and theory. In his "Definitions" Jung writes: "Fantasy as an imaginative activity is, in my view, simply the direct expression of psychic life, of psychic energy which cannot appear in consciousness except in the form of images and content." (*Collected Works* 6, ¶ 722).

Jolande Jacobi, one of Jung's closest collaborators, who also worked intensively with pictures, collected some 4,500 pictures by patients of C.G. Jung, painted between 1917 and 1955. The Archive also contains about 6,000 works from Jolande Jacobi's own practice. These pictures were stored and categorized under the watchful eye of Jungian analysts such as Jolande Jocobi, Rudolf Michel, Michel Edwards, Cecilia Roost, Paul Brutsche, Vicente de Moura, and Ruth Ammann.

The Picture Archive is often sought out by people interested in the creative work of patients and in active imagination, the method C.G. Jung developed and applied as a form of therapeutic work with inner imagery. The present curator of the Picture Archive, Ruth Ammann, had the idea of presenting a selection of these invaluable works on the 70th anniversary of the C.G. Jung Institute in Zürich. The selection of pictures was to be published and accompanied by several essays dealing with various aspects of the collection. Verena Kast and Ingrid Riedel welcomed the idea, and Ulrich Peters, the head of the publishing house Schwabenverlag AG, and Christiane Neuen from the affiliated Patmos publishing house also caught on to the idea of an illustrated book publication.

The pictures were also to be exhibited in a museum space. We were delighted that we were able to win over Monika Jagfeld, the curator of the Museum im Lagerhaus, Foundation for Swiss Naïve Art and Art Brut, St. Gallen, who agreed to organize an exhibition in her museum. This publication includes the pictures that were shown there and thus documents the exhibition.

On behalf of the two other editors, Ruth Ammann and Ingrid Riedel, I would like to express my sincere thanks to all the authors for their contributions. I am also indebted to Christiane Neuen and Ulrich Peters for designing the lovely German language edition and to the Susan Bach Foundation for their generous support for that edition.

For the Editors
Verena Kast
President of the Board

In the Land of the Imagination

THE C.G. JUNG COLLECTION

Monika Jagfeld

The Picture Archive of the C.G. Jung Institute

THE ENTIRETY OF PICTORIAL works that the psychiatrist and founder of Analytical Psychology, C.G. Jung, collected from his patients was shown to the public in the "Museum im Lagerhaus" in St. Gallen between March and July 2018 for the very first time. It is a long-kept treasure that the C.G. Jung Institute Zürich, Küsnacht, presented to a wider audience on the occasion of its 70th anniversary, which happened to coincide with the 30-year anniversary of the "Museum im Lagerhaus" in the same year.

The collection comprises about 4,500 works, mainly paintings, but also drawings and embroidery, created between 1917 and around 1955.[1] The artists remain anonymous, with their works sorted by 105 case numbers. Several pieces had previously been shown at exhibitions, and a selection of mandalas was on display at the Oglethorpe University Museum of Art in Atlanta, Georgia, in 2012. The opportunity to gain an overall impression of the collection, however, had not been possible until 2018.

There are only a small number of this kind of collection, usually compiled by doctors at their respective psychiatric institutions and clinics. Well-known examples are the Morgenthaler Collection at the Psychiatric Museum Bern/Waldau in Switzerland or the Prinzhorn Collection at the Psychiatric University Hospital Heidelberg in Germany. While psychiatrist Walter Morgenthaler collected the artistic works of his patients who were hospitalized at Waldau, the artwork of psychiatric patients from the entire German-speaking area was sent to Hans Prinzhorn at the clinic in Heidelberg. A doctor and art historian himself, he proceeded to categorize the pieces from a scholarly point of view.[2]

Some key aspects, however, distinguish the C.G. Jung Collection from historic art collections of psychiatric institutions. Jung's patients were not hospitalized but came to see him as private patients in his practice, which he had opened in Küsnacht on Lake Zürich in 1909. Hence, the prerequisites for artistic creation and material procurement were different from the very outset, as was the impulse for this kind of activity.

Patients in institutions worked individually and mostly of their own accord, without therapeutic guidance or motivation. Many works reflect the personal incapacitation and confinement, as well as the loss of living space, possessions, and identity that their creators experienced in the clinics. Seen from this perspective, art did not serve as a means of therapy, but rather offered a tool for survival and the possibility to create a new identity, adapted to a new reality of life.

All of this was not of concern to Jung's private patients. Their works cannot be considered a reflex to some form of loss, but rather an expression of a deeper exploration of the self, embedded in the therapeutic setting. They were certainly part of a therapeutic process and came into being because of Jung's encouragement to visually formulate inner pictures and characters that would subsequently be discussed with and analyzed by him. But only because they did not originate as an independent art form, does this mean that they should not be seen as art in their own right?

In the Rapture of Mythology

As a matter of fact, the C.G. Jung Collection is one of its kind and cannot be compared to any other collection of his professional colleagues at the time. There are similarities between the works and Jung's own pictures in his *Red Book* that he created over a period of sixteen years, between 1914 and 1930. The explanations in the *Red Book* are therefore rather revealing with a view to his patients' pictures.

The *Red Book* is at the core of Jung's self-experiments in which he confronted his inner pictures and fantasies that he initially recorded in his diaries, the so-called Black Books. These sketches were later transcribed in calligraphic form to the *Red Book*, where they were complemented with painted, "materialized" pictures. In this process, he saw himself more as an alchemist than an artist, while he discovered that his dreams and fantasies - similar to those of his patients - were inundated with mythological imagery and contained motifs that indeed paralleled alchemy.

More still, he deliberately excluded art from this process as he felt that the unconscious was part of the natural realm and not the artistic one.

> People said: "He has an artistic temperament." But it was only that my unconscious was swaying me. Now I learn to act its drama as well as the drama of the outer life [...].[3]

> I once asked myself, "What am I really doing? Certianly this has nothing to do with science. But then,what is it?" Whereupon a voice within me said, "It is art" This made the strangest sort of impression upon me, because it was not in any sense my impression that what I was writing was art. Then I came to this "Perhaps my unconscious is forming a personality that is not I, but is insisting on coming through to expression'." I don't know why exactly, but I knew to a certainty that the voice that had said that my writing was art had come from a woman. ...
>
> Well, I said very emphatically to this voice that what I was doing was not art, and I felt a great resistance grow up within me. No voice came through, however, and I kept on writing. I then suffered a second shock, similar to the first one: 'It is art.' This time, I caught her and said: 'No, it is not' and I felt as though an argument would ensue.[4]

Jung's confrontation with his inner pictures and fantasies was an intense interaction with the collective unconscious and it certainly changed his analytical work. He encouraged patients to undertake similar self-experiments by guiding them through Active Imagination, asking them to allow inner pictures to emerge. They learned how to induce visions in a waking state,[5] lead inner dialogues, and paint their fantasies. The goal was to "try to get into the picture, to become one of the actors." Jung demanded that "you must be in them more, that is you must be your own conscious critical self in them - imposing your own judgments and criticism."[6]

A female patient remembers:

> In those early days, when one arrived for the analytic hour, the so-called *Red Book* often stood open on an easel. In it, Dr. Jung had been painting or had just finished a picture. Sometimes, he would show me what he had done and comment upon it. . . . The master thus demonstrated to the student that psychic development is worth time and effort.[7]

In this way, the pictures in the C.G. Jung Collection "show the development of many an analytic treatment and the symbols of this process. Moreover, there are pictures and documents which illustrate what Jung's patients experienced during the therapy." writes Vicente L. de Moura (cf. his article in this book).

It was important for Jung that archetypes be recognized as such, and he considered the mandala one of the best examples for an archetype's universality (cf. Verena Kast's article in this book). There was evidence for him that "these things – mandalas especially – really are produced spontaneously and were not suggested to the patient by my own fantasy."[8] The mandala as a symbol for the center of the personality was therefore placed in the exhibition's gallery, with the pictures arranged closely side by side to surround and circle around the visitors in an attempt to move them - and their selves - into the center.

Locations, Topics

Apart from the mandala and its related symbols, further striking motifs are repeatedly found both in Jung's *Red Book* and the works of his patients: the snake, the sun, light, water as the bubbling water of life, and in the form of floods, ships accompanied by water (case 010), the tree of life, passageways, the world egg - and again and again, the human being. Visionary, cosmic illustrations stand next to animal and landscape paintings, grotesques next to surreal-fantastic scenes. For Jung, someone without access to their own myth was "uprooted, having no true link either with the past, or with the ancestral life which continues within him, or yet with contemporary human society."[9] Seen from this perspective, the pictures serve as footholds and locations. The exhibition attempted to bundle topics in such a way that they comprised several cases to illustrate topical parallels, expressed in various forms of presentation. This book discusses the picture series at great length, and it was likewise presented in the exhibition in an attempt to deepen the process of Active Imagination in an exemplary manner.

"The sleep of reason gives birth to monsters" is inscribed on one of the sheets of the "Caprichos" (1799) of Francisco de Goya. Similarly, Active Imagination seems to have triggered some awkward and eerie creatures in Jung's patients (cases 037, 050, 064 or 034), or the unconscious emerged on the canvas as an ominous black cloud (case 105).

Personal conflicts and fears create individual demons. The woman is often at the core of these "subjective mythologies." In line with Jung's direction to "try to get into the picture, to become one of the actors," these sheets were obviously created by women. Sexuality and the body, sexual and physical identity, as well as motherhood were important topics and further central themes of the exhibition.

In this context, contradictions between Jung as the therapist and analyst and his patients became obvious. The latter articulated concrete emotional wounds in their artwork, which Jung then transcended into archetypal concepts. The illustrations of the captivated, fettered, crucified woman (cases 026, 034, 056, 055) are disturbing, and the symbolism of violence in a sexual context is equally threatening (e.g. the extensive series of case 105).

One sheet of case 064, stored as a photo in the Picture Archive, focuses on the analytical process itself (064, CLAC): Unprotected and naked, a woman is kneeling on a blanket, opposite a hovering magical circle, its beams burning a deep hole into her body. But the hole has the shape of a large, receiving ear, out of which beams are leading back to the circle that could also be regarded as an eye. The patient titled her work "Analysis."

Another case (No. 041) illustrates living history between the years 1939-1947, triggering pictures of infernos that bear witness to the trauma of an entire war generation (cf. Ingrid Riedel's article in this book).

In this way, the collection conveys contemporary references and aesthetic influences of C.G. Jung, as well as artistic impressions of Art Nouveau and Symbolism. Some of the dark monsters allude to sheets by Odilon Redon or Alfred Kubin (case 034), while Modernism is reflected by the reduction and abstraction in the picture series of cases 009 and 042. There is also evidence of a connection between the Dada Movement and the "Psychological Club" founded by Jung in the same year (cf. Doris Lier's article on case 009 in this book). The sheets of case 004 or 026 reflect an affinity to Surrealism, while the illustrations of case 067 refer to Hermann Rohrschach's inkblot pictures; several botanical drawings reflect Karl Blossfeldt's aesthetic photographs (cases 012 and 018).

To be sure, the quality of the works varies, depending on the patients' skills and talents, who – as amateur artists - usually dared to elaborate their Active Imagination in visual form. At best, we could be astounded by many of the pictures' high quality. In addition to the ones mentioned above, the works of case 019 merit particular attention. Their spherical visions and opulently entwined mandalas in subtle watercolors have not only been put on paper, but also realized in delicate embroidery.

"The *Prima Materia* for a Lifetime's Work"

The creation of the *Red Book* was a central topic for C.G. Jung:

> The years when I was pursuing my inner pictures were the most important time in my life—in them, everything essential was decided. . . . The later details are only supplements and clarifications of the material that burst forth from the unconscious, and at first swamped me. It was the *prima materia* for a lifetime's work.[10]

C.G. Jung's *Red Book* was first shown in New York in the fall of 2009 and published as a facsimile the same year. At the Biennale in Venice in 2013, its presentation in the "Il Palazzo Enciclopedico" exhibition of curator Massimiliano Gioni caused a sensation. Five years later, in 2018, the C.G. Jung Collection was on public display at the "Museum im Lagerhaus" in St. Gallen for the very first time. It is documented in this book, which also served as an exhibition catalogue. While the *Red Book* was described by C.G. Jung as "the *prima materia* for a lifetime's work", the exhibition can be regarded as its addendum and continuation. "I understood that my dreams and my visions came to me from the subsoil of the collective unconscious," remarked Jung in an interview in 1952. "What remained for me to do now was to deepen and validate this discovery."[11] The C.G. Jung Collection offers outstanding material for new discoveries. Similar to the *Red Book*, it may surprise the audience anew and attract a comparable level of attention.

Notes

[1] The Picture Archive consists of four collections, including the Jolande Jacobi Collection of around 6000 works of patients, cf. Vincente L. de Moura's article in this book

[2] Cf. Prinzhorn, Hans, *Artistry of the Mentally Ill. A Contribution to the Psychology and Psychopathology of Configuration.* 2nd edition. Springer, Berlin, 1995.

[3] Jung, quoted from: Sonu Shamdasani, "*Liber Novus: The Red Book* by C. G. Jung." In: Jung, C. G.: *The Red Book. Liber Novus.* Edited and with an Introduction by Sonu Shamdasani. Preface by Ulrich Hoerni. Philemon Series. W.W. Norton & Company 2009, 216.

[4] Id.: *Analytical Psychology,* 70, quoted from: ibid., 199.

[5] Cf. Shamdasani: "*Liber Novus,*" 215.

[6] Quoted from: ibid., 217.

[7] Keller, 205.

[8] Shamdasani, 220.

[9] Jung, Foreword to the Fourth Edition. In: *Collected Works* , Vol. 5, 38.

[10] Id.: *Memories, Dreams, Reflections,* 244.

[11] Id.: Combat Interview, 1952, quoted from Shamdasani, 201f.

References

Jung, C. G., *Memories, Dreams, Reflections.* Recorded and edited by Aniela Jaffé. Special edition. Fontana Press, London, 1995.

— —., Foreword to the Fourth Edition. In: *Collected Works* (CW) Vol. 5: *Symbols of Transformation. An Analysis of the Prelude to a Case of Schizophrenia.* 2nd edition, Bollingen Foundation Inc. NY, published by Princeton University Press, Princeton NJ, 1956.

Keller, Tina, C. G. Jung: Some memories and reflections. In: *Inward Light* 35, 1972, 1-18.

Prinzhorn, Hans, *Artistry of the Mentally Ill. A Contribution to the Psychology and Psychopathology of Configuration.* 2nd edition. Springer, Berlin, 1995.

Shamdasani, Sonu: *Liber Novus: The Red Book* by C. G. Jung. In: Jung, C. G.: *The Red Book. Liber Novus.* Edited and with an introduction by Sonu Shamdasani. Preface by Ulrich Hoerni. Philemon Series. W.W. Norton & Company 2009.

Making the Inner Word Visible

THE PICTURE ARCHIVE AND ITS HISTORY

Vicente L. de Moura

The beginning of the last century was marked by tremendous upheavals in Europe. The political, economic and cultural transformations shook the very foundations of society and everywhere one had the sense that it was the dawning of a new age. The discoveries, theories, and experiments in science, such as Einstein's theory of relativity or the X-ray image introduced new perspectives that put the old-world order into question. It was believed as if anything would be possible thanks to science. Such changes also led to great insecurity: traditional structures were questioned, and social tensions could be felt. What was once held to be secure had suddenly lost validity.[1]

This epoch also witnessed experiments with dreams, visions and fantasies. The boundaries between literature, art and psychology were not clearly delineated yet and the search for new paths, new ways of understanding, perceiving and shaping society assumed diverse forms.[2]

In this period of radical changes Jung began his work as assistant doctor at the Burghölzli Psychiatric Clinic in Zürich, one of the most renowned and progressive institutions of psychiatry in this period. Looking back, Jung described the psychiatric landscape of the time which, in his view, was governed by scientific materialism – a dogma that viewed psychic disturbances as disorders of the brain. Possible psychic aspects were hardly taken into account in their etiology.[3]

Jung experimented and studied under the direction of Eugen Bleuler. He conducted the word association experiments and was thus able to show on an empirical basis that there exists a level beyond consciousness, namely the unconscious, that influences behavior. Based on this finding, he presented his complex theory and obtained recognition for his scientific work. However, Jung became disappointed about the limitations of focusing on statistic processes in psychiatry and thus increasingly turned to other therapeutic methods. In this connection his encounter with Sigmund Freud was significant. Jung, in fact, was convinced Freud introduced psychology to psychiatry.

The two met in 1906 and continued to develop and propagate psychoanalysis. However, due to theoretical and personal conflicts the cooperation between the two pioneers came to an abrupt end in 1913. In his subsequent phase of disorientation

Jung noticed that his scientific work had been one-sided until then and – in keeping with the spirit of the times – had only taken rationality, use and value into account.[4]

In 1913 and 1914 Jung had a series of dreams and visions on catastrophic events in Europe – dreams that he was unable to understand. At first he thought that he was on the verge of succumbing to a mental illness. But once World War 1 erupted he concluded that the dreams and visions had not referred to him but rather had been a sort of premonition of a collective phenomenon.[5] Jung was not alone in experiencing such premonitions about an imminent catastrophe in Europe. Shortly before 1914 prophesies regarding an apocalyptic war were in the air and works on this theme abounded in art and literature.[6]

Active Imagination Evolves

In order to understand what had happened to him Jung began carrying out a series of experiments. His "most difficult experiment,"[7] as he put it, was his experimentation with his own fantasies and then his attempt to grasp the experiences he had. He delved into his innermost fantasies, documenting them, and conducted dialogues with his inner figures in a kind of dramaturgical play of imagination. First, he processed the resulting material first in a literary way and later he transcribed the texts over a period of years in calligraphic form in the so-called Red Book and added elaborate drawings. However, it is important to note that Jung's experiments were comparable with other experiments taking place at the time, as for instance those conducted by Herbert Silberer[8] who studied the emergence of inner Picturery in a trance-like state or those of Ludwig Staudenmaier[9] who experimented with the personification of inner figures. (Jung knew and quoted Silberer's experiments in his publications.) As mentioned above, such experiments were very common in the early 20th century.[10]

This approach to the inner world enabled Jung to find a way out of the labyrinth of unconscious Pictures. He discovered that his engagement with his inner world and the creative expression thereof was helpful. Later this process became an important part of his method. He dubbed it active imagination.

The Beginnings of Jung's Work with Pictures

From 1916 onwards, Jung encouraged his patients to engage in a dialogue with their inner figures, the personifications of their psychic complexes. Later he motivated them to give creative expression to their dreams, inner experiences or active imaginations in the form of drawings, paintings, embroideries, sculptures, dances, etc. He noticed that his patients were thus able to find a way to process their psychic experiences and to integrate their conflicts and the elements of their inner world – in a way that enabled them not to feel fragmented or split.

The patients reported their fantasies and dreams to Jung and brought him their pictures. Jung analyzed them and supported the patients in their inner dialogue. Since Jung did not want his patients to remain without their pictures, some of them made him copies of their drawings so that he was then able to study them in-depth later.[11] This is how a collection of pictures gradually came into being – a collection that also included notes that patients made about their Pictures that evolved during their work with Jung.

Jolande Jacobi and the Foundations for Today's Picture Archive

In the late 1950s Jolande Jacobi began systematically cataloging the Pictures that had accumulated – no easy task. However, the collection of pictures, a very valuable one no doubt, was difficult to categorize because of the lacking uniformity. Jacobi suggested first defining the purpose of the collection as well as the criteria for the selection of Pictures.[12] Later, she created a card index so as to identify the Pictures according to motifs and symbols. The material was divided again into four collections. The first collection comprised some 4,500 pictures from Jung's patients and well as patients of a small group of analysts (a total of about 50 cases). The second collection comprises pictures by Jacobi's patients (about 6,000 pictures) and the third group of pictures mainly has photos of paintings and sculptures with archetypical motifs (today this collection is part of the ARAS – The Archive for Research in Archetypical Symbolism). The fourth collection is made up of photographs from the so-called "Eranos Collection" – a collection started by Olga Fröbe-Kapteyn who organized the first Eranos conferences in Ascona from the 1930s on – and this collection includes black-and-white photographs of archetypical motifs from alchemy, art and antiquity.

006 AFAI · Anonymous, undated
Watercolor on paper
Picture Archive, C.G. Jung Institute Zürich-Küsnacht

In his last years Jung gave the collection to the C.G. Jung Institute and the pictures archive became a research center for the interested public and students of Jungian psychology. Following Jacobi many other analysts have contributed to organizing the pictures archive. The curators of the institute have, apart from their main tasks such as teaching and research, also ensured that the pictures were adequately conserved and restored. The material in the archives also includes information about the patients from various sources, but Jung himself did not leave any systematic register of his patients.

The additional information in the archive is thus very enlightening, since in some cases it describes the context of Jung's therapeutic work. This allows one to see the space in which the pictures emerged, their *temenos* – the sacred space – and the context of the picture also becomes clear. In the 1980s and 1990s, Michel Eduards, supported by Cecilia Rost, systematically ordered the collection. They classified Jung's cases, dated them (when possible), gave each picture an identification number and added keywords for easier search. Eduards also began entering information by electronic means, photographing the pictures and capturing them on slides so as to conserve the material and elucidate the historical background. Most recently, the holdings of the pictures archive were digitalized, which has simplified handling of the material and the access to it.

The pictures archive reveals the history of many encounters with the unconscious. It is the largest, most significant collection of pictures and related comments from Jung's patients. The study of these pictures gives us insight into how Jung himself viewed these pictures. They show the development of many an analytic treatment and their symbols in the process. Moreover, there are pictures and documents, which show what Jung's patients experienced in the therapy. To exemplify this, I would like to present a picture that, in my view, is very enlightening.

Therapeutic Work with Pictures – an Example

In the 1930s Jung treated a Dutch woman who was born in the Far East. René J. van Helsdingen described her case in Beelden uit het Onbewuste published in 1957. When she began treatment with Jung, she was suffering from panic attacks and was able to find comfort and relief in drawing. In the preface to this book Jung wrote the following:

> The pictures are artistic compositions in the positive sense and are uncommonly expressive. They communicate their frightening, demonic content to the beholder and convince him of the terrors of a fantastic underworld. (...)The pictures not only illustrate that phase of treatment that brought the contents of her neurosis to consciousness, they were also an instrument of treatment, as they reduced the half conscious or unconscious Pictures floating about in her mind to a common denominator and fixated them. (...) The therapeutic effect of this technique consists in inducing the conscious mind to collaborate with the unconscious, the latter being integrated in the process. In this way the neurotic disassociation is gradually remedied.[13]

In this quote Jung addresses the underpinnings of his therapeutic understanding in the work with pictures. According to the patient's description, in this picture she showed Jung the underdeveloped parts of her personality that are depicted around her (034 BHAW). She found it shocking that the picture revealed how unbalanced she herself was.

034 BHAW · Anonymous, undated
Charcoal on paper
Picture Archive, C.G. Jung Institute Zürich, Küsnacht

The picture also shows other elements of the treatment, e.g., how the patient may have experienced Jung's interventions in the analysis as well as aspects of the transference. It is important here to underscore the words "may have", since each interpretation is a hypothesis. In the center of the picture stands the patient who is looking at her inner figures, i.e., her complexes. Jung is standing behind the patient and holding her. His stance can be seen as supportive but also as encouraging her to engage with what she sees. The confrontation with the self is a central aspect of the analytic work and often results in a certain sadness, as one can see in the patient's facial expression. Jung's stance seems to be: look there! That's it, that's what you are!

Jung is the source of light in the picture – a reference to the transference element of this patient, the projection on Jung of a beyond-human element – a 'mana personality' that brings light into darkness. The projection of an archetypical figure onto the therapist can often appear as part of analysis. The picture clearly shows how this patient experienced it. It also reveals that, for this patient, Jung had a 'trickster', i.e., a playful, shrewd side. The trickster-element is the "fox" on Jung's forehead.

Van Helsdingen describes how the patient was confronted with her own immaturity and how she had to realize that she had neglected her inner life and that many parts of her personality were underdeveloped. The various complexes are portrayed in the following pictures: the corpse of a witch whose eyes have been gouged out by a two-headed eagle; the prostitute who is raped by a pig; the mummy mother (as this figure was called by the patient herself); the subservient male servant and the dead tiger. The description and interpretation of these symbols would go beyond the scope of this essay but their visual depiction offers us unique insight into the patient's inner life. The therapeutic effect of painting and the discussion of the picture as part of the therapeutic relationship shows clearly how it affected her and testifies to the effectiveness of Jung's method. In his books Jung writes that the psyche, the inner world is real and that their reality becomes visible in pictures. This shows how important it is to take pictures seriously, to engage with them and to take to heart what they express.

Such pictures and many more can be viewed in the pictures archive. The first drawings are from 1917, a time in which Jung was still occupied with his own self-experiment with the imagination. Many others followed over a span of more than forty years. The main goal of the archive is to support the study of picture interpretation and archetypical symbolism. What began as an experiment developed into a therapeutic method – a method that helps us to engage with the inner world. Seen in this light, the pictures archive is the result of C.G. Jung's work with his fantasies. It makes the inner world visible in a creative way. The pictures testify to an effective method of treating psychic conflicts. In the picture archive we can learn, study, let ourselves be inspired and experience the history of Analytical Psychology.

Notes

[1] Cf. P. Blom, *The Vertigo Years: Europe, 1900-1914.* Basic Books: New York 2008.

[2] Cf. Sonu Shamdasani, Liber Novus: The "Red Book" by C.G. Jung. In: Jung, C.G.: *The Red Book. Liber Novus.* Ed. & Introduction by Sonu Shamdasani. Preface by Ulrich Hoerni.

[3] Cf. C.G. Jung In: *Collected Works*, Vol. 3:

[4] Cf. C.G. Jung, *The Red Book.*

[5] Cf. Shamdasani, The "Red Book" by C.G. Jung, 203.

[6] Cf. Ibid., 200.

[7] C.G. Jung, *Black Book* 2

[8] Silberer, Herbert: Bericht über eine Methode, gewisse symbolische Halluzinations-Erscheinungen hervorzurufen und zu beobachten (1909). In: *Jahrbuch für psychoanalytische und psychopathologische Forschung*, Vol. 1, ed. Eugen Bleuler/Sigmund Freud. Franz Deuticke: Zürich/Vienna 1909, 513-525.

[9] Ludwig Staudenmaier, *Die Magie als experimentelle Naturwissenschaft.* Sarastro: Paderborn 2012.

[10] Cf. Shamdasani, *The Red Book* by C.G. Jung.

[11] Cf. C.G. Jung, On the Foundations of Analytic Psychology. *Tavistock Lectures* (1935). In: *Collected Works,* Vol. 18..

[12] Cf. the memo of Jolande Jacobi dated June 21, 1956, *Dokumente des Bildarchivs*, C.G. Jung-Institute Zürich.

[13] C.G. Jung, Foreword to van Helsdingen "Beelden uit het onbewuste" (1954). In: *Collected Works*, Vol. 16.

009 AIBB Anonymous, untitled, 1917

From Non-Sense to Primordial Sense

ECHOES OF DADA IN THE PICTURE ARCHIVE

Doris Lier

The Pictures

THE HOLDINGS OF THE picture archive at the C.G. Jung Institute include a series of pictures, only part of which has been accessible to the public, comprising works that were painted by a woman in 1917, 1918/19 as well as 1928/29.[1] These are among the earliest pictures to be found in the archive. Altogether there are 32 sheets of different sizes, with one of C. G. Jung's analysands named as the artist.

Fifteen sheets are introduced on a separate cover sheet: "PICTURES/ FROM MAY 22/ 1917/ TO HIM WHO BROUGHT THEM TO TO LIGHT./" Each of the fifteen sheets is numbered on the lower right-hand edge from I to XV.[2]

Apart from the pictures dated May 22, there are three other pictures that do not feature any Roman number on the right-hand side; only the year "1917" is noted. There is also one picture from 1917 with a number VIII. A further sheet marked with"1917 or 18" obviously could not be clearly attributed; it seems to have been dated later.

In another seven pictures one finds "IX 1918", "II 1919", "III 1919" and ""V 1919" on the bottom right-hand side, with "V 1919" appearing in three different pictures.[3] Whereas the pictures dated May 22 belong together, the dating and sequence of the following pictures leave questions unanswered and there also seem to be several pictures missing.

Nine years later, beginning with "IV 1928", the 'artist'/analysand apparently made another go at it, but now only four pictures were created; perhaps only four remain. The third picture shows the exact date "4.11.1928," the last one the year 1929. Here, too, Jung's analysand added the numbers and dates herself.[4]

So much for the archival details. Now what is actually depicted in these pictures?

The Motifs and Style of the Pictures

The partial series of May 22, 1917 that comprises fifteen pictures can be divided, both in formal terms and thematically, into four sequences. The first sequence with four pictures shows a stiffly standing, fetish-like figure without legs and feet.[5] Four sheets follow in the second sequence, each sheet depicting a mandala that is oriented either inwardly or outwardly by a snake.[6] The next sequence with three further sheets is completely dominated by the snake, which seems to have

Series of May 22, 1917

Series from 1917 to 1919

Series from 1928/29

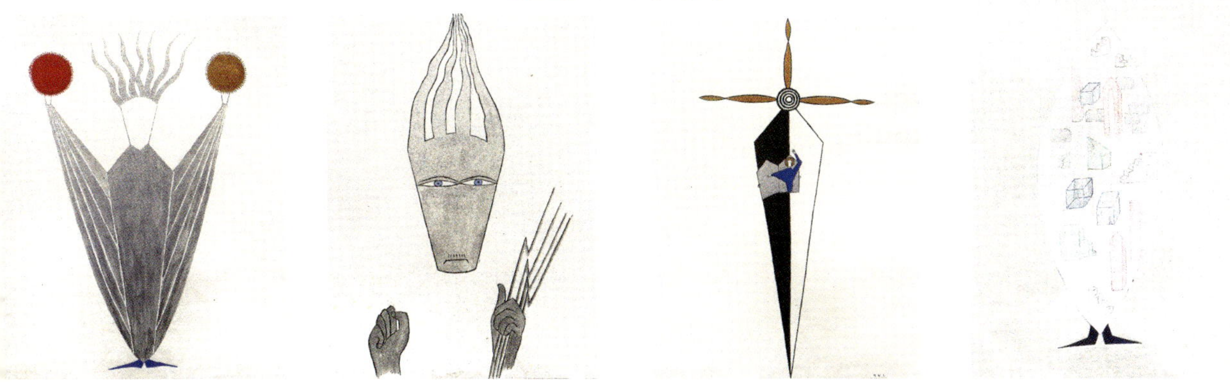

009 AIAW

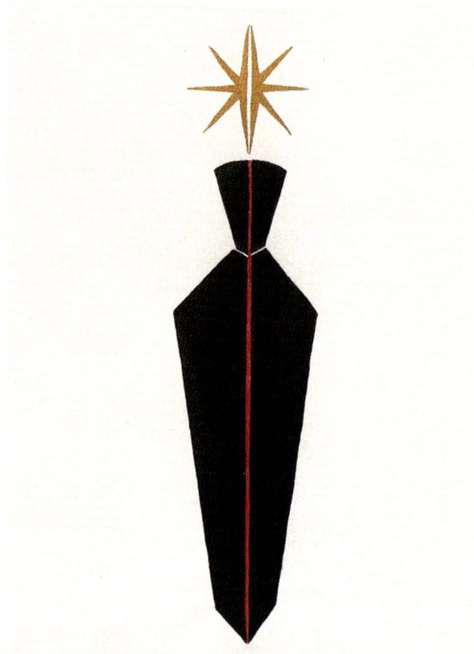

009 AIBA

009 AIBB

009 AIBC

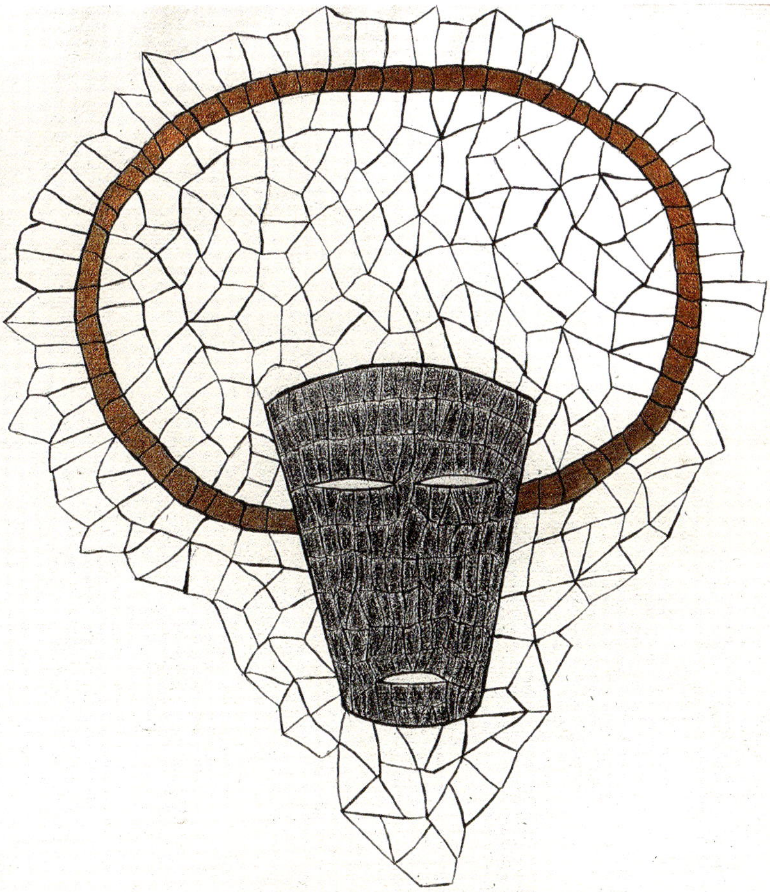

009 AIAT

liberated itself from the mandala and now roams freely. The last sequence with four sheets depicts a plant-like, then tree-like formation with seven arms, resembling the tree of life. It first emerges from the serpent, yes, is begotten by it, then it stands on a ball floating in the water; in the next picture it appears to be threatened by water snakes and finally, having become stronger, succeeds in vanquishing the water snakes. All of these drawings are highly stylized, with the formal and chromatic impact becoming increasingly intense. In seven of the fifteen pictures a mask-like head appears, first as the head on the four little figures, then as the head of the snake. The mask is always conical, tapering off towards the bottom. In all of the pictures this head has only eyes and mouth, but no nose. Four times it dons a fan-like headgear, which lends it a special dignity.

On the twelve other sheets from 1917-1919 the motif of the little fetish-like figure and that of the mask are taken up again. The mask is occasionally shown with a headgear but now it assumes different forms. Four times it appears with a body, once embedded in a honeycomb-like background and once in the center of a rectangular background filled with tiny masks. In several instances, the figure is without a face. The little figure always features a mask in lieu of a head. In contrast to the May series in which it simply stands in an empty room it is now integrated in a picture setting and in 1918/1919 arms, hands and once even small feet are added. A snake appears to have wound itself around the figure, then the figure appears in different scenes: pierced by wooden sticks, standing upright between sun spheres, stretched out on a wheel that features hands on its spokes, balancing on top of a blue ball, and with a brown ball rising up from it.

The late series from 1928/1929, which only consists of four pictures, once again takes up the mask and the little figure, but now a shade of light gray prevails so that the pictures appear noticeably paler. Here the last figure is especially noteworthy: only a stylized body is depicted, replete with cubist elements, and now it no longer has a mask.

Here, however, two black feet stand out, as if the figure was just about to exit the scene. The little feet were already alluded to in 1919, in the picture in which the figure is standing on top of a blue ball.

What is so striking about these pictures is the continuous stylization and the presence of classical Jungian symbols – circle, ball, wheel, snake, sun and water. The *Red Book*[7] immediately comes to mind; here, similar motifs, painted by Jung himself, can be seen. What is also striking is the frequent appearance of the archaic mask. It appears 22 times in a total of 32 pictures, which allows us to infer their great importance for the woman undergoing analysis. (009 A1AT, previous page)

Masks do not appear so often in *The Red Book*. When they do, they look completely different.[8] The masks painted by the woman in analysis with Jung were most likely, inspired by Dada and archaic cultures. The Dada movement, which began in Zürich in 1916, was certainly the talk of the town at the time most of the pictures were made, 1917 to 1919. As for the concerns of the movement and how it related to analytic psychology, this will be briefly explored in the following.

Dada: The Destruction of Values

On the occasion of the opening in Cabaret Voltaire on Spiegelgasse in Zürich, Richard Huelsenbeck, one of the fathers of Dada, explained what the movement wanted:

> We want to change the world with nothing, we want to change poetry and painting with nothing and we want to bring an end to the war with nothing." To this end "adult men and women" donned "strange cardboard rolls on their head, elicited primal sounds, jumped around like machines and proclaimed nonsense with great conviction" as the editor of the *Dada Almanac*, H.M. Compagnon noted.[9]

The members of Dada were fiercely determined to create crazy, non-sensical artworks and to perform in the Cabaret Voltaire. But certainly, as alluded to above, not "out of the blue" or as "l'art pour l'art." Their protest against any kind of sense or meaning was dead serious. They sought to wage a war against war with peaceful-artistic means. It was the middle of the horrific World War I and in Zürich – the place where many artists and intellectuals sought refuge – exile art was to be created. Art reflecting indignation towards values, since values, as the creed said, were behind every war.

The main founders of the Cabaret Voltaire were Hugo Ball and Emmy Hennings from Germany. And their best known comrades in arms were: Tristan Tzara and Marcel Janco from Romania, Richard Huelsenbeck from Germany, Hans Arp from the Alsace and – not much later – the Swiss artist Sophie Taeuber.

They experimented loudly with "nothing," in pictures and in writing, with different materials, styles, and forms. Tristan Tzara formulated instructions for composing a Dadaist poem: words were to be cut out of an article, placed in a bag, which was to be shaken, and the words were then arbitrarily recomposed. Text Pictures, sound and simultaneous poems emerged in this and similar ways.

Jung and Dada: A Mesalliance?

From what has been said thus far it is clear that Jung and Dada do not go together. Dada stands for nonsense, for a systematic rejection of meaning. Jung looks for archetypal imagery and, by extension, for the meaning of psychic states, no matter how confusing they appear.[10] The Dada movement sought to mitigate the suffering brought on by World War I through artistically formed destruction of the world.[11] Jung seeks to discover primordial values in 'a priori' ideas which structure the images of the psyche.[12] Jung was thus not able to derive anything from the Dada movement.

Yet there were many Dadaists who found sources of inspiration for their new art in Jung (as well as in Freud)—it is here that one sees the first links.[13] This hardly comes as a surprise. Where, if not in the unconscious, do the imaginations lie hidden, those that could ridicule ideal principles? And how, if not through 'free association', could something irrational and absurd be extracted from the unconscious?

The relationship between Dada and Jung seems to have been one-sided. The Dadaists, it seems, exploited Jung and Freud so as to enrich their denial of values with strange ideas from the unconscious.

Yet the psychic affinity between Dada and Jung is stronger than it may seem. Even in terms of time, there were coincidences: In February 1916 Dada was founded in Zürich's old city center, only shortly before the "Psychological Club" located in the nearby Gemeindestrasse was established. This could just be a coincidence and thus irrelevant, yet there is clear evidence "that the events that took place at the Psychological Club and Dada Zürich often shared their audiences."[14] Jungian analysts were friends with Dadaists and Erika Schlegel, the librarian of the Psychological Club, even appeared at the Cabaret Voltaire, together with her sister Sophie Taeuber. Jung himself reported there were patients who "didn't draw but rather danced mandalas."[15]

Dada: A Yearning for Primordial Beginnings

Dada was, on closer scrutiny not just about protest. In the tumultuous presentations at the Cabaret Voltaire, the "Soirées nègres," it mainly targeted European values. With drums and mask dances from Africa, Australia, Oceania, and Latin America, everything that smacked of bourgeoisie was to be destroyed. The originality of archaic cultures was a main bearer of hope.[16] The yearning for primordial beginnings concealed the idea of reactivating original values and developing new formal idioms. "Jolifanto bambla o falli bambla" – that is not just nonsense but alludes to African rhythms. Hugo Ball, dressed in his famous cubist bishop costume, kept reciting the poem titled "Caravans" at the Cabaret Voltaire "until he seemed to be in a state of trance and had to be carried off stage."[17] The shenanigans were more superficial and contained, initially perhaps in a concealed way, a utopia of regression.

Sophie Taeuber and Hans Arp as Representatives of a Mystic Dadaism

Sophie Taeuber and Hans Arp played an eminent role in the Zürich Dada scene. They had known each other at least since 1916 through the Cabaret Voltaire and from the beginning they were closely linked in their artistic work.[18] Taeuber, a painter, sculptress, textile designer, architect, and designer, born in 1889, preferred archaic, geometric elements; she shared these with Hans Arp and also continued to develop them together with him. In 1918 she made the first of their famous "Dada heads." She was inspired by the Hopi Indians for whom masks played a major role.[19]

Since 1908 Hans Arp worked arduously to develop new forms of representation. That same year he wrote that he had withdrawn into solitude "so as to struggle 'with abstract art like Jacob with the angel' and at the same time to rid himself of his academic training."[20] He named his creations "mandalas," "moving ovals," or "navels."[21] In 1916, Hugo Ball noted "Arp's infatuation with the circle and cube," in formal simplicity and clarity, "that which is still untouched by European civilization."[22] Three years later Arp and Taeuber read works by C.G. Jung at the sanatorium in Arosa.[23]

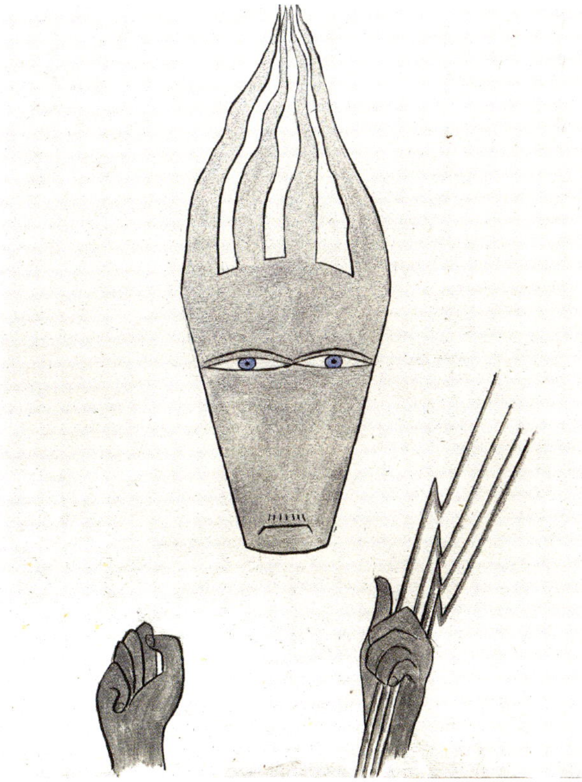

009 AIBF

The Picture Series: An Attempt at an Overall Interpretation

"TO HIM WHO BROUGHT THEM TO LIGHT." To whom is this dedication of the first 15 drawings directed? The pictorial symbolism, which also appears in *The Red Book*, allows us to infer that this person is C.G. Jung. He was the one who began to show his patients his own experiments with what he was describing as the collective unconscious in this time and asked them "to imitate what he was doing." He also offered "to support them while they were experimenting with their own stream of inner pictures."[24]

It can be assumed that the woman in analysis with Jung was really happy to accept his invitation and felt very indebted to him. She tried, one could say, to assimilate the wish of the person who had brought her pictures to light. Perhaps this connection was the reason why the mask, amazingly, shows a moustache three times, e.g., in 009 A1BF.

The very close connection with Jung must be taken into account in the interpretation. The pictures cannot simply or not simply only be understood as spontaneous phenomena rising up from the collective unconscious. They also reflect

009 AIAM

009 AIAN

009 AIAO

009 AIAP

an intense transference process and the adoption of the healing path offered by Jung.

The last four pictures of the series from May 22 reveal classical individuation symbolism. A tender plant is born, then receives earth and water; next, it is threatened by water until, having grown stronger, it is able to confront the water serpents. (009 A1AM - 009 A1AP)

Since all fifteen pictures were created on one single day we cannot assume that the woman who drew these pictures herself traversed the individuation path in a few hours. A related development probably took place earlier; but perhaps the motif is also largely borrowed. This immediately triggers off alchemist associations, which had taken on ever-greater significance for Jung since his break with Freud and had served him as models of the individuation process.[25]

So much for the Jung's strong influence on his female patient in these first fifteen pictures. The archaic figure, in particular the mask-like head in many other pictures, can be understood as an influence from the Dada movement, which, in the non-European, archaic sculptures did not just seek nothingness but was rather drawn to original forms and values and with them a new beginning. Even the formal reduction of the drawings to a bare minimum was inspired by Dada, in particular by Sophie Taeuber and Hans Arp The yearning for one's origins is the link connecting Dada, Jung, and the patient who drew these pictures.[26]

As I interpret them, the pictures are not just simply spontaneous manifestations emanating from the collective unconscious but, first and foremost, products of transferences. To be sure, there was personal suffering in the background. This is something that can hardly not go unnoticed in several of the pictures created between 1917 and 1919. The little figure that never relinquishes its stylized character, is portrayed so that it reflects suffering and hope, mortal injury and resurrection. The patient was probably torn between extreme states, between painful questioning and feelings of resurrection, with optimism becoming more

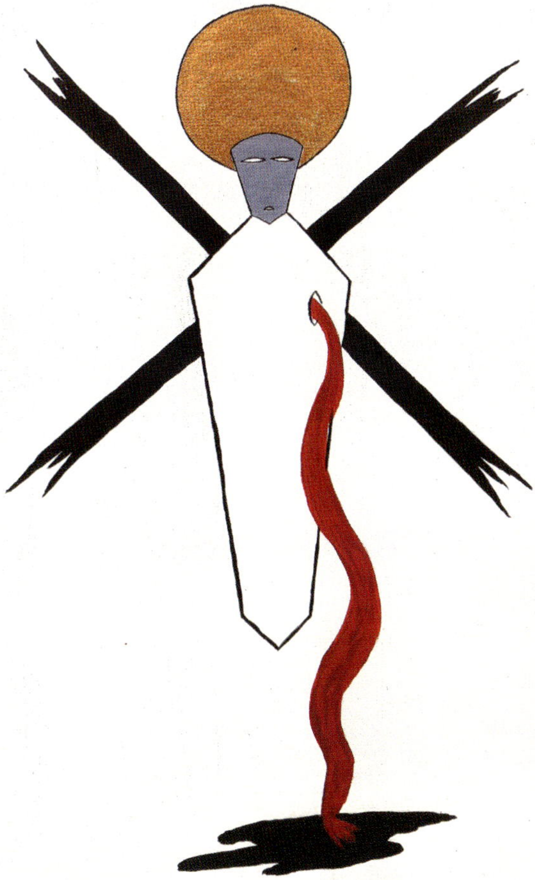

009 AIAS

009 AIAX

pronounced towards 1919. (009 A1AS and 009 A1AX).[27]

Several pictures contain an antithesis, that is, they can have both a positive and negative meaning. This is particularly striking in the representation of the figure stretching his arms on a sort of wheel with spokes on the tip of his hands. (009 A1AX)

What at first glance appears to be a crucifixion can also be understood as an expression of a sense of tension in a greater whole. However, the facial expression seems to be more indicative of suffering.

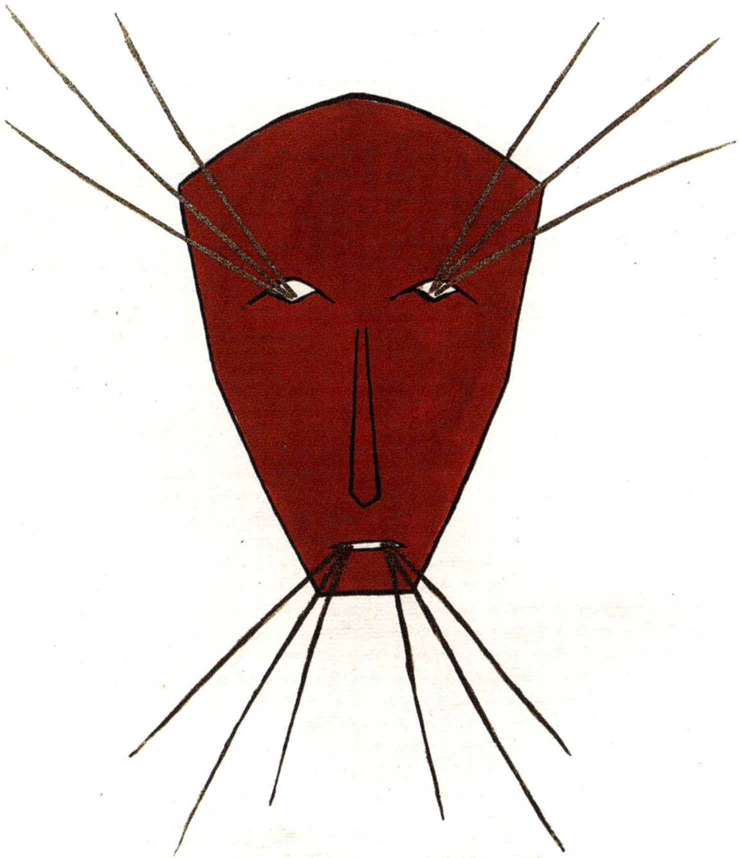

009 AIAQ

A mask that was created in 1917 is similarly ambivalent, with rays or arrows leading from or to its eyes and mouth (009 A1AQ). This picture, too, triggers a sensation that is unsettling, but when the lines are understood as rays it can also be perceived as hopeful.[28]

There seems to be no doubt to me that the woman (who was in analysis from 1917 to 1919) was in a severe psychic crisis, I would even say: an identity crisis. She tried to cling to Jung and Dada (perhaps only to individual representatives of the Dada movement, most notably Sophie Taeuber

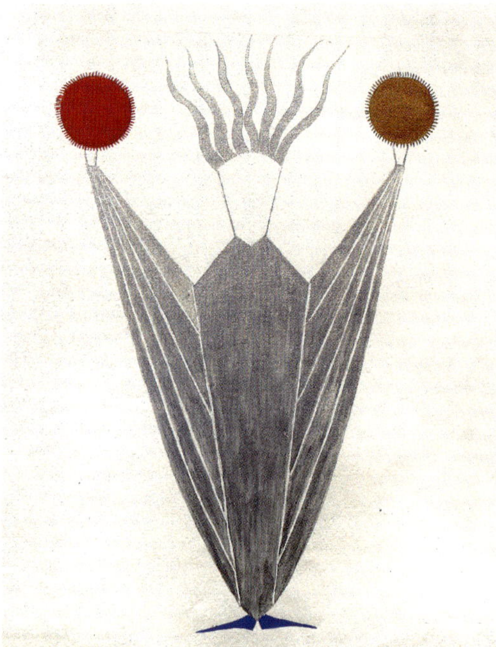

009 AIBE

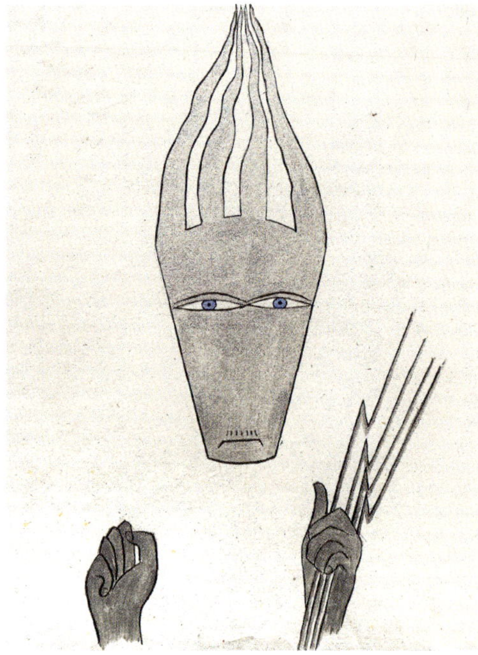

009 AIBF

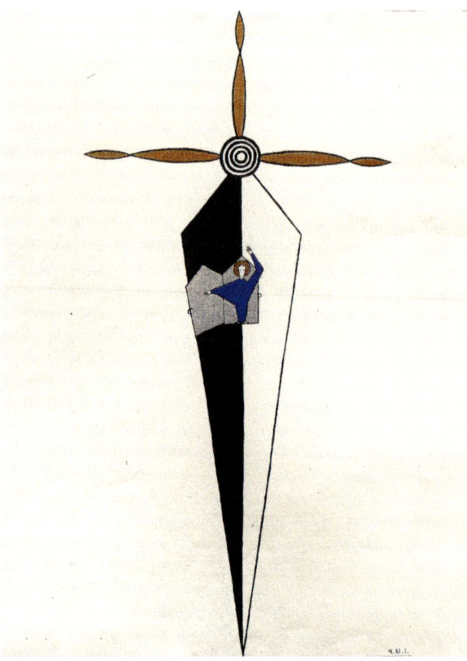

009 AIBG

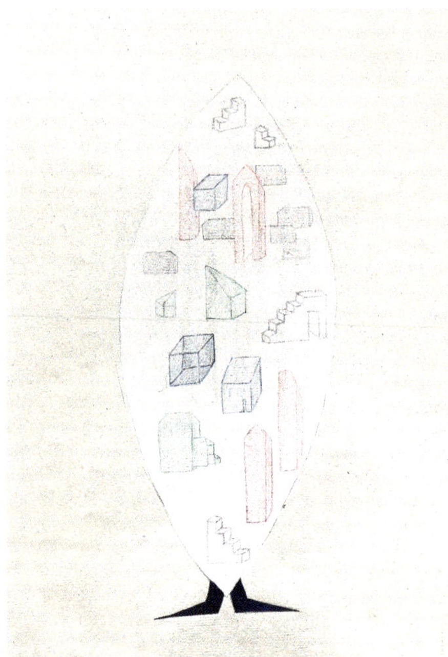

009 AIBH

and Hans Arp), experiencing the focus on simple, clear forms as salutary and healing. Seen in this light, Jung the analyst as well as representatives of the Dada movement served as models and figures of identification, temporarily assuming the role of an auxiliary ego in this woman's psyche.[29]

The recourse to archaic forms can also be read as an attempt to project personal suffering on to primal forms and motifs and to thus make it tolerable. Personal suffering is in this sense transferred to a general and primordial human dimension and thus kept at bay. Thanks to elementary forms of representation suffering can be understood as the *conditio humana*. Stylizations also reflect the same wish: they integrate the individual in a basic, eternally valid and thus perfect order[30]

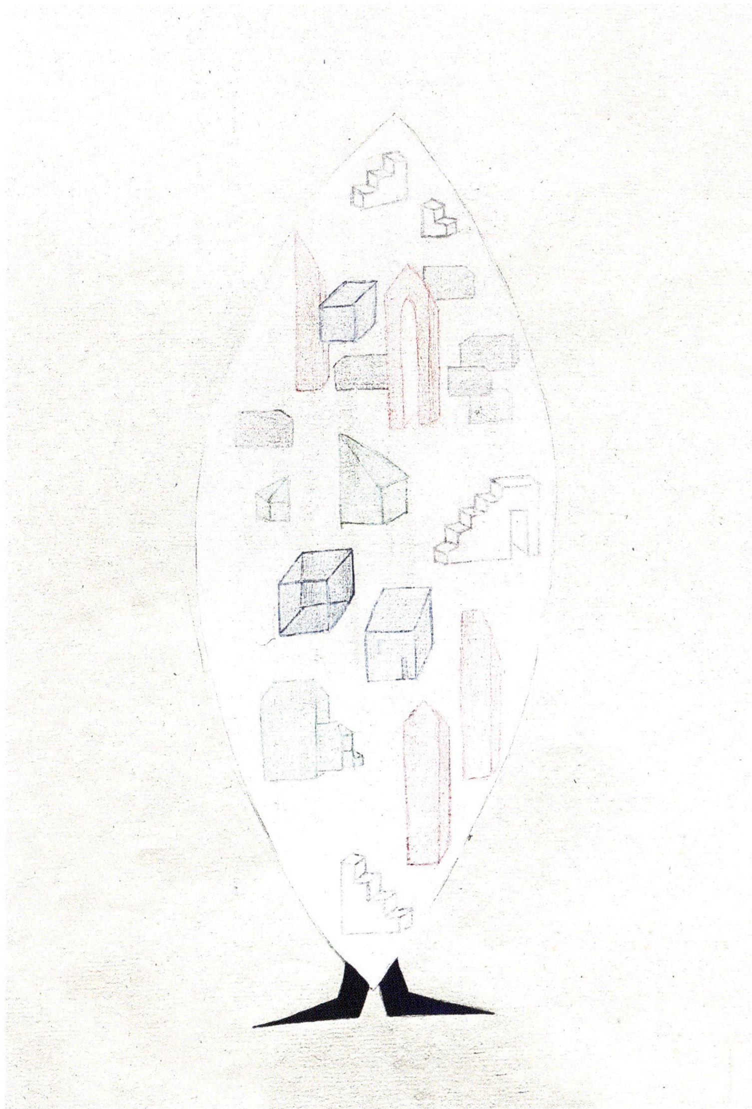

009 AIBH

In the last "series" of 1928/29 (009 AIBE - 009 AIBH)– that is nine years later – the colors light gray, black, and white prevail as has already been noted.

The last picture, 009 A1BH, shows cubist forms in the process of dissolving within a stylized body. The affinity with Dada is once again underscored in this figure. However, the black feet, which immediately stand out as a contrast to the pale colors, could indicate that the ongoing path has come to an end and the woman in analysis is now ready to go her own way without the influence of Dada and archaic models – perhaps even without Jung.

Notes

[1] I am grateful to Ruth Ammann, who has been responsible for the Picture Archive for some years now, for letting me see these pictures.

[2] It is quite amazing that 15 pictures and a cover sheet were created in one single day.

[3] "11 1919" could also be "1 1919." A correction was made here so that it is no longer clear which of the two it is.

[4] The sheets are of different sizes – something I did not take into account in my study. It seems as if the analysand used sheets that happened to be available.

[5] It is not easy to discern the sex of these figures. Two of the four are probably female. Perhaps the artist was referring to the human being in a general sense.

[6] The first mandala is modeled after the previous figures in the sense that the upper part resembles the bust-head of the previous figures.

[7] C.G Jung, *The Red Book. Liber Novus.* Ed. (with introduction) by Sonu Shamdasani. Philemon Foundation & WW Morton & Co 2009.

[8] Cf. In *The Red Book*, masks generally have an animal form or show demonized human features.

[9] *Dada-Almanach.* Vom Aberwitz ästhetischer Contradiction. Textbilder, Lautgedichte, Manifeste, eds. Andreas Puff-Trojan and H.M. Compagnon. Manesse, Zürich 2016, 127.

[10] C.G. Jung, "On the Archetypes of the Collective Unconscious" 1934/35, CW 9/1, ¶16 and ¶66.

[11] "The Psychological Aspects of the Mother Archetype" 1938, CW 9/1,¶ 155.

[12] CW 10, ¶ 44

[13] Rainer Zuch, *Die Surrealisten und C.G. Jung.* Weimar: VDG, 2004.

[14] Ibid., 219f.

[15] Ibid., 263.

[16] "Dada Africa" was the name of the exhibition that took place at the Rietberg Museum on the occasion of the 100th Anniversary in 2016. In this exhibition the "Back to primordial beginnings" is present throughout.

[17] *Dada Afrika. Dialog mit Fremden.* Ed. Ralf Burmeister et.al. Scheidegger & Spiess, Berlin 2016, 10.

[18] Cf. Zuch: *Die Surrealisten und C.G. Jung,* 264f.

[19] Like the masks of the woman who created this drawing, these masks are often without a nose. Cf. illustrations and creations by Sophie-Taeuber and Hans Arp, also in: *Dada Afrika.*

[20] Zuch, 217, with a quote from Arp, Hans: *Unsern täglichen Traum. Erinnerungen, Dichtungen und Betrachtungen aus den Jahren 1914-1954.* Verlag der Arche, Zürich 1955, 7.

[21] Ibid., 250.

[22] Ibid., 249f.

[23] Ibid., 222.

[24] Sonu Shamdasani. In: Jung, *The Red Book, 217.*

[25] The pictures are best interpreted as a manifestation of Pseudo-Democritus' formula: "Nature rejoices in nature, nature vanquishes nature, nature reigns over nature." Cf. *Alchemie. Lexikon einer hermetischen Wissenschaft,* Beck: Munich 1998, 109.

[26] In addition to works by Sophie Taeuber and Hans Arp, works of the Hopi Indians and ancient Egyptian sculptures will have served the analysand as a model in her drawings. A precise stylistic analysis would be informative.

[27] As already stated, it is not entirely clear what the sequence of the pictures is.

[28] The wheel as well as the rays that lead to and away from the face are symbols that play a major role in Niklaus von Flüe.

[28] The wheel, like the rays pointing to and away from the face, are symbols that play an eminent role in Niklaus von Flüe.

[29] Here I'm using the auxiliary ego-concept not in the sense of Moreno's psychodrama but in the sense of Annelise Heigl. See: Heigl-Evers, Annelise / Ott, Jürgen: *Die psychoanalytisch-intellektuelle Methode.* Theorie und Praxis, Vandenhoeck & Ruprecht, Göttingen 1995.

[30] On stylization or aesthetization see also: Jung, C.G.: *Memories, Dreams, Reflections.* Recorded and edited by Aniela Jaffé. Corrected special edition. 19th edition, Edition C.G. Jung im Patmos Verlag, Ostfildern 2016, 210.

References

Alchemie. Lexikon einer hermetischen Wissenschaft. Beck, München 1998.

Arp, Hans: *Unsern täglichen Traum. Erinnerungen, Dichtungen und Betrachtungen aus den Jahren 1914–1954.* Verlag der Arche, Zürich 1955.

Dada Afrika. Dialog mit dem Fremden. Hg. von Ralf Burmeister et al. Scheidegger & Spiess, Berlin 2016.

Dada-Almanach. Vom Aberwitz ästhetischer Contradiction. TextPictureer, Lautgedichte, Manifeste. Hg. von Andreas Puff-Trojan und H.M. Compagnon. Manesse, Zürich, 2016.

Heigl-Evers, Annelise / Ott, Jürgen: *Die psychoanalytisch-interaktuelle Methode. Theorie und Praxi*s, Vandenhoeck & Ruprecht, Göttingen 1995.

Jung, C.G.: Erinnerungen, Träume, Gedanken. Aufgezeichnet und herausgegeben von Aniela Jaffé. Korrigierte Sonderausgabe. 19. Aufl. Edition C. G. Jung im Patmos Verlag, Ostfildern 2016.

— —.: *Die psychologischen Aspekte des Mutterarchetypus* (1938). In: GW 9/I, §§ 148–198.

— —.: *Das Rote Buch. Liber Novu*s. Herausgegeben und eingeleitet von Sonu Shamdasani. Vorwort von Ulrich Hoerni. Einleitung, Hinweise des Herausgebers zur Edition, Anmerkungsapparat und Danksagung aus dem Englischen übersetzt von Christian Hermes. Philemon Series. 4. Aufl. Patmos, Ostfildern 2016.

— —.: *Über die Archetypen des kollektiven Unbewußten* (1934/35). In: GW 9/I, §§ 1–86.

— —.: *Über das Unbewußte* (1918). In: GW 10, §§ 1–48.

Shamdasani, Sonu: Liber Novus. Das „Rote Buch" von C.G. Jung. In: Jung, *Das Rote Buch*, S. 195–223.

Zuch, Rainer: *Die Surrealisten und C.G. Jung.* VDG, Weimar 2004.

065 CMAB, DETAIL. Anonymous, untitled, 17. 8. 1935
Gouache on paper, 31.5 × 49.5 cm
Image Archive, C.G. Jung Institute Zürich-Küsnacht

Finding One's Own Center

THE SYMBOLISM OF MANDALAS

Verena Kast

The Mandala

MANDALA, A WORD THAT stems from Sanskrit, is generally translated as circle, holy, circle or even as magical circle. In Tibetan Buddhism, mandalas are used as objects of meditation and concentration and as such are linked to an ancient spiritual tradition. In Buddhism mandalas have a magical or religious meaning, focusing primarily on a deity.

A mandala is seen as a figural or geometric diagram; it is usually square or round and directed towards a central point. In a simple version the mandala can be a triangle but in its more complex, intricate form it can also represent the momentary perception of the entire universe. Structurally, it establishes order and harmony, and in terms of content, stories are told—about one's own life and about life in general. The design of the mandala, often also in the form of sand pictures, is central to Buddhism. These mesmerizing, moving sand pictures, executed with great concentration and care, are subsequently destroyed to reflect the ephemerality of the material world. This should also highlight the role of the meditative composition, the creative process and, to a lesser extent, the final product.

In Western civilization "mandalas" generally seen as circular designs focused on a central point, depict geometrical, figural or even plant-like motifs. They can also be meditative pictures with a similar structure as the Eastern mandalas and have a calming effect.

C.G. Jung's Approach to Mandalas

In 1918/19 C.G. Jung served as "Commandant de la Région Anglaise des Internés de Guerre" in Chataeux d'Oex. In *Memories, Dreams, Reflections*[1] he describes how every morning he would make a little circular drawing, a kind of mandala, in his sketchbook. "My mandalas were cryptograms of the state of my self which were presented to me anew each day. In them I saw the self—that is, my whole being—actively at work. (...) The self, I thought, was like the monad which I am, and which is my world."[2] Jung noted that the self came into being in these mandalas, the entire personality, the connection of the unconscious and conscious mind, as is possible in this sense, that the "goal of psychic development is the self. There is no linear evolution; there is only the circumambulation of the self."[3]

In 1927 Jung dreamt of a mandala that he then

proceeded to paint.[4] At the time Richard Wilhelm sent him the manuscript of "Secret of the Golden Flower."[5] This text enabled Jung to discover the connection of his mandalas with the Eastern mandalas. The symbol of the mandala represents the integration of aspects of one's own psyche but also aspects of cultural and social life.

In Jungian psychology dissonances in the psyche can be overcome by means of symbols. And one of the possible ways of overcoming a dissociation is to design a mandala. In my view the mandala is not simply an expression of the Self; like all symbols it has emerged from the tension between an individual's present life context, the background of his or her life and the unconscious dynamic. I also see mandalas as being the result of emerging processes that are assimilated and structured, and elaborated with great care until they assume optimum form.

Jung did not just devote a lot of thought to the "growing over" of conflicts and dissociations. Again and again he would point to the dissociative nature of the psyche, especially in connection with the theory of complexes. The individuation process is not just about the experience of wholeness; it also about enduring, understanding and reflecting on the existing oppositions. This is also true for the composition of mandalas. This idea does not detract from the meaning of a genuine mandala, experienced from within. It also shows that the mandala has its legitimate place in certain life situations and does not simply lead to individuation or it is not necessarily an expression of individuation.

Mandalas—A Product of the Therapeutic Process

Jung was influenced by the Tibetan mandalas, just as he himself had an influence on his patients. Jung writes the following about his patients' mandalas:

> They are (...) tools of meditation, reflection, concentration and the realization of inner experience (...). At the same time, they also serve to create an inner order and are thus often found when they appear in picture series immediately following chaotic, disorderly, conflicting states accompanied by anxiety. The thus reflect the idea of a safe refuge, of inner reconciliation and wholeness.[6]

Jung saw them as a "self-healing attempt of nature."[7] But he also distinguished these pictures from cultic mandalas. He noted that individual mandalas show "a plethora of motifs and symbolic allusions"[8] they seek to express the entirety of an individual in the experience of his inner and outer world or an important inner point of reference to this experience. Its subject is the self as opposed to the ego, which is only the point of reference for consciousness, whereas the self encompasses the totality of the psyche, namely the conscious mind and the unconscious."[9] If anything at all it is the possible expression of the Self at a particular moment—and not the Self *per se*.

The Circle and the Center

Of course, we do not just find the circle in mandalas.[10] However, the mandalas created by Jung's patients, which I have selected here, are all dominated by the circle, bordered by a circle which probably serves to contain the spontaneous imaginations that emerged while they were being created. There is probably also a spontaneous compositional principle at work here, which responds to aesthetic demands, finding expression in the painting of the mandalas. Likewise, It is conceivable that the fascination of the mandala, as an archetype of wholeness, had an influence on the design—possibly even as a consequence of being emotionally affected by Jung, as noted by the 'painters' in therapy with him. Yet this does not change the fact that C. G. Jung kept this method under wraps for many years so as to avoid suggestion. [11] Jung will have certainly been keenly aware that something kept secret often has a greater impact on reality than something clearly visible. What speaks in favor of an emotional "contagious" effect is that mandalas appear much less frequently today than they did in Jung's time —and this even in persons who do a lot of painting in the therapeutic process.

The circle and the spirals related to the circle are ancient symbols used by people. They are very common, everyday forms. We circle, en-circle something important. This means that we want to direct our attention to it in the future as well. The circle is an endless line, without a beginning or an end and can be drawn in one single movement without pause. The circle represents something round, self-contained - wholeness. And the circle encloses the interior. The line of a circle delineates the 'inside' from the 'outside'. What is inside is shielded, protected. For this reason, one speaks of a nurturing circle; in ethnology it is also seen, for instance, as offering protection against demons—demons being something we feel threatened by.

The circle is closed, the manifold aspects of the outside world are excluded and one is content with what is at hand. You can concentrate. Each circle has a center and this center reveals what is central in a particular moment. The center, as we learn from the circle, cannot be lost. The center also enables movement—an extension and expansion but also a movement upwards and downwards—the circle extending to become the symbol of a ball. When we focus on ourselves, collect ourselves, then the section of experience, too, becomes 'round' - we feel contained in something round—and whatever we do is protected. The circle reproduces the experience of a primordial containment and whatever happens in the circle or is depicted here, is a part of this primordial containment. However, the creative process also requires dedication, care and focus on what can be seen in imagination. Something round also evokes gentleness, which can be reflected in the tender care of gentle work.

According to Panksepp the primary process emotional systems are simply "given", part of our basic biological make-up, of our collective unconscious; they can be inhibited or activated by later life experiences but they are basically present and something we share with the animal world. Of these systems we could say that curiosity and interest for what is encircled is linked to wanting to understand and design. In the language of the affective neuroscientist Panksepp it is about the "SEEKING system and the CARE system. The CARE system is the emotional foundation of mothering and nurturing, on the basis of which the pro-social feelings develop."[12] If the SEEKING system and the CARE system are actually activated by painting in a circular form, then it would be possible to create significant resources against fear and sadness. Painting in a circle—even without the division into quarters that mandalas often contain—could have a therapeutic effect in providing a shelter for development. Here one must also examine the form of imagination. A different form of imagination could appear in a circle: one that relates to a center, to something central—and this in a sheltered space. This reference to the center is perhaps only possible in painting, in creating mandalas. In this sense the mandala can really serve as the "traditional antidote for chaotic mental states"[13] but, as I have just described, it is certainly much more. It is the concentration on imagination, which involves something of central importance—perhaps not just related to current personal questions but also to more universal life issues. One should not forget that the symbol of the circle and also that of the spiral has played an important role in the designs of humans since the beginning of time. Just think of the circles found on old stones, the circles made of stones, the circles and spirals on sarcophagi. It is always about life and death, the reference to the finite and the infinite. But let us first think of the first drawings by children, with their primordial, circular forms, as in 'tadpole' figures.

Examples of Mandalas

One first preliminary note: We know neither the life story nor the life situation of the patients who painted these mandalas. It is thus impossible to interpret each of these mandalas, that is, to relate them to a given life situation, to aspects that point into the future or even to find references to the therapeutic relationship. We also do not know whether all of these mandalas were painted as part of a therapeutic process with Jung. Of course they can also be understood from the relationship to C.G. Jung as being a gift to Jung, depending on the type of transference. We give you what is important to you—and that is also important to us. And perhaps also: we do everything to back your theory and your importance also makes us become important. We do not know for sure. These mandalas, painted with great care and dedication, are copies that were made especially for C.G. Jung, that is to say, were meticulously painted a second time, reproduced from the original, so that he would have a copy. Jung felt that the painter should keep the original.

Second preliminary remark: Mandalas are there to be looked at, for contemplation. And if we are touched by a mandala, similar themes are activated in our psyche—perhaps the theme of finding one's center is also addressed—and in the best case we are motivated to paint our own mandala. Here we should also think about how mandalas actually emerge, that is, how emotions generate certain imaginations[14]—emotions that are unconscious; the special figures, shapes, etc. stem from everyday experience. Similar to our dreams, in

025 AYBC · Anonymous, untitled, undated
Gouache on on Paper, 14 x 14 cm
Picture Archive, C.G. Jung Institute Zürich-Küsnacht

our imagination new perspectives of experience, memories and expectations often result from the often unusual, unexpected combinations of these figures, shapes, pictures.

Growth and Transformation

The painter is an approx. 30-year-old American woman. In the seminar reports for the German Seminar of 1930[15] Jung reported in-depth about her visions—he called them 'imaginations' at the time. Her personal life story, to the extent it is known, is not taken into account here—the seminar reports only make fleeting reference to it in. Today we would be more interested in finding out in what life situation and therapeutic relationship these imaginations and especially the mandala in question (Archive No. 025AYBC) were created. However, it is interesting that the patient developed this Picture from an imagination. First, there was the imagination, which was described in great detail in the seminar. From this imagination the painter selected this one motif—a number of other motifs would have been possible—and by painting it she also changed the motif—resulting in this very mandala.[16] A three-fold creative process has taken place: first the imagination, then the selection of the Picture that she wanted to create and then the elaboration of if, in the course of which the inner Picture continued to change as we know from internal pictures—it is always about creating and re-creating, elaborating and re-elaborating, giving creative form to something. In this one Picture in particular, it seems that the imagination was a kind of preparation, while the Picture then was a kind of condensation of the theme and also a temporary solution to the conflicts—in the mandala. In reference to the elaboration of other mandalas, Jung did not speak of imagination but of automatic painting. Generally speaking, Jung called the act of painting a form of active imagination.[17]

The viewer's gaze is drawn to the center. In the innermost of three circles a child is visible—still in a fetal position but with its hand visibly opened—on a ground of violet, a color of transformation. This child—symbolizing something that will become new in the painter's life—already has a hand that is ready to grab something (the hand being ahead of the embryo's stage of development). The number three defines the mandala: three circles, three snakes, and the three expresses dynamism. Something is moving here, and it can be integrated in one's current life. The child in the innermost circle shows five allusively stretched fingers and the number five is symbolically linked to the body and thus also to the real physical world.

The innermost circle is delineated in black, contained by three golden circles. Violet and yellow-gold are the colors of complementarity—a contrast is balanced out here. The three light-green serpents do not touch the innermost circle, they are also not coming from the outside. They can be understood as an activating energy, as transformative energy. In the imagination snakes are nourishing the embryo. As a symbol, snakes stand for energy, for ambivalent, pressing emotions from the unconscious. Here they do not seem ominous; the green color connects them more to growth impulses from the unconscious as a sign of transformation. Transformation basically stands for the dynamic of death vs. life and this, too, is symbolized by the snake. What does this mandala convey? There is something new in the center, a promise driven by a significant unconscious impulse, connected with a striking transformational dynamic, that is something emotionally very alive. This impulse is contained by the structure of the mandala, the three circles and by the colors used in the mandala. Here there is certainly a lot of psychic energy and emotional movement but it can all be integrated in everyday life.

008 AHAC

008 AHAD

008 AHAF

Dynamic from the Egg

The following pictures (Archive Numbers 008 AHAC, 008 AHAD, and 008 AHAF) were created by an approximately 60-year-old patient who was considered to be artistically gifted by C.G. Jung. But in this connection it is more significant that Jung also speaks of a "blocked individuation process", pointing out that it was the therapeutic process that stimulated the patient's creative activity.[18] Here, too, 008 AHAC) the center draws attention: in the middle the egg is surrounded by a wreath, which in terms of colors harmoniously unites fire and water. The oppositions are integrated—and the egg is given the necessary warmth to brood. At the same time, there is also a form of stimulation, which represents inspiration. The process of maturation is contained, shaped—but also emanates onto a calm background, into greater, universal dimensions. This could be understood as a personal process of maturation, concentration on the creation of a new personal world but also as a possibility for such personal experiences to emanate onto others.

The egg as a symbol: From mythology we are familiar with the world egg, representing "great roundness"—the egg that contains the entire cosmos. But also in the ordinary chicken egg there is potential life. The egg is thus seen as a symbol of fertility. To mull, brood over something also means to give a development the necessary time and the necessary warmth—concentrating on the center as the brooding of something that is tantamount to a world emerging, a new understanding of one's own world, ideas replete with meaning for the future. This Picture must be seen together with following one (008 AHAD). What is growing out of the egg?

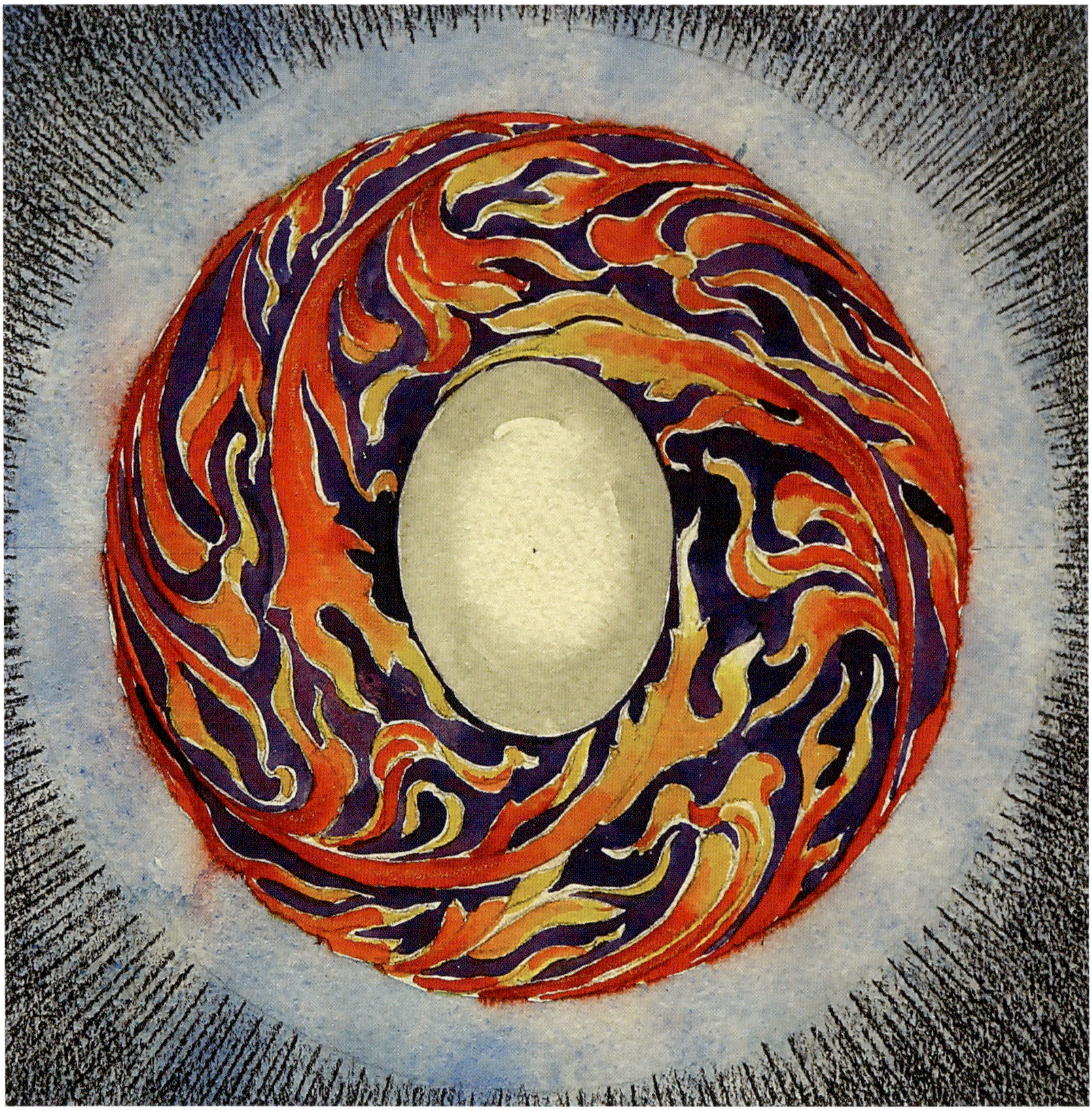

008 AHAC · "The Hatching of the Egg" ("Das Ausbrüten des Eis")
Gouache on on Paper, 16.5 x 16.5 cm
Picture Archive, C.G. Jung Institute Zürich-Küsnacht

008 AHAD · "The First Tree of Life from the Egg" ["Der erste Lebenbaum aus dem Ei"]
Gouache on on Paper, 31 x 21 cm
Picture Archive, C.G. Jung Institute Zürich-Küsnacht

008 AHAF · "The First Tree of Life from the Egg" ["Der erste Lebenbaum aus dem Ei"]
Gouache on on Paper, 31 x 21 cm
Picture Archive, C.G. Jung Institute Zürich-Küsnacht

A kind of tree is springing forth from a blue circle in the violet-colored center. The painter has titled this picture "The first tree of life from the egg."

The tree of life can be seen as a symbol of the process of individuation over the course of time, of life-long development and maturation. Here, too, it still appears as a first premonition just as the egg did. But it is no longer only about finding one's center, but also about assimilating new developments from the center and perceiving them, activating the process.

In this picture, too, we find water and fire again. Here, however, the fire hat not been extinguished; instead the tree has both water and little flames – it is a kind of fountain that also disseminates light but everything is still very tentative, muted. Fire and water move with all their polarities: the dichotomies can be contained and thus produce a living Picture, a living emotional experience. Enthusiasm, also something whimsical, can be experienced, both of which have emerged through contact with the unconscious—and also through the work with C.G. Jung, through the fire that was kindled in the therapeutic process. It is the first tree of life—a first fantasy of what could be essential to life—and the fantasies here are still quite innocent. There are the little flames and the pink blossoms, all of which looks a bit like art deco—in contrast to the powerful, emotional composition at the bottom of the tree where a greater, more intensive vitality can be noted. The third dimension has merged from the two-dimensional mandala, thus enabling the Picture to extend into life, a new dimension of experience. The tree growing out of the mandala perhaps also shows the painter how inner experience can be brought to bear on outer reality, to embody it in everyday life.

What attracts me is the center with the dynamic flames shooting up from it. An emotional creative force emerges from the egg—be it emotionality, emotional intensity, sexuality or creativity or what have you. Here there is no more waiting and brooding but rather action and the pleasure derived from this, as shown in the mandala.

The next picture (008 AHAF) shows the circle in a large dynamic—centered in a snail house or a shell. Dynamic and calm, enthusiasm and stillness are linked. The snail house (or is it a shell?) has the effect of keeping the painter from being carried away by the dynamic. The picture conveys a movement of curling inward and the dynamic is, once again, directed towards a calm center, resulting in a successful connection of oppositions. This picture brings home the extent to which mandalas can serve as containment, a secure holding which we also see as the effect of a positive mother archetype or as a product of the CARE system. What is striking is the eye of the fish—a second center? What does it see from its perspective? A powerful dynamic emerges from the unconscious. The fish is what "fires"—a content of the unconscious—still in the guise of an animal, but it cannot be overlooked. But in the center one recognizes the house of a snail or a shell, finely drawn, a silent growth, a calm sense of being at ease with oneself.

The Inner World Emanating to the Outside

Jung described the painter as a middle-aged patient. The title the painter gave the picture was "Bright Sun." (002 ABAC) This mandala mainly shows a structural and figurative composition, but its content

002 ABAC · "Bunte Sonne" ["Colorful Sun"]
Anonymous, colored pencil on paper, 15 x 17 cm, 1931
Picture Archive, C.G. Jung Institute Zürich-Küsnacht

is not illustrated with pictures; the entire mandala depicts a sun. This mandala was drawn with a compass. Here the yellow stands out—and with it, together with the title, the light, the warmth, the emanation. In the center there is a white circular form which clearly emanates in the shape of a cross. What is being experienced in the center radiates out into the world, not only into the white, but also the radiation into the red, which resembles the lightly swirling arms of a windmill. When the viewer focuses on the mandala, with its static structure, the radiating colors lend the Picture a dynamic. The fifth circle is particularly interesting; it is structured by the colors red, green and blue and it is the circle of everyday life. What is experienced in the center emanates into everyday life, making it more radiant. But this radiance extends way beyond everyday life. There is still the not very complete, fraying circle, which extends beyond the fifth one. This is a mandala that centers, establishes order in the understanding of the world, while at the same time expressing the hope that what is being processed on the inside will transcend the personal world.

Final Remarks

Even if these mandalas move us, and perhaps even trigger our own inner pictures, we cannot really access the emotional experiences of the patients who drew the mandalas. Let's not forget that both the imaginational and the compositional processes were linked to everyday conflicts, to interpersonal experiences and, in particular, to what was experienced in the therapeutic relationship with C.G. Jung, to the focus on inner development. A long, dramatic process has come to a tentative end with the successful elaboration of a mandala. This experience could be accompanied by an overwhelming sense of having solved important issues for the time being and having reached closure with oneself and the world, a sense of satisfaction with one's life and being able to reflect on it with awe. Such experiences –sensing a connection with oneself, with others, with something that is greater than oneself—are the result of a long, often arduous psychotherapeutic process, but also a promising sign that such a harmonious situation may arise again in the future.

Notes

[1] C.G. Jung, *Memories,Dreams., Reflections.* Recorded by Aniela Jaffé, trans. from the German by Richard and Clara Winston, Vintage Books Edition. Toronto: Random House: 1989, 220.

[2] Ibid., 221

[3] Ibid., 222..

[4] Described as picture 6 in: C.G Jung, Concerning Mandala Symbolism, *Collected Works*, vol. 9:1, ***Archetypes and the Collective Unconscious,*** Bollingen Edition, Princeton, N.J. Princeton Univ. Press, 1980./ Wilhelm, Richard: *The Secret of the Golden Flower: A Chinese Book of Life,* trans. and explained by Richard Wilhelm, with a commentary by C.G. Jung.

[5] Ibid.

[6] Jung, *Collected Works 9:1,* §710.

[7] Ibid., §714.

[8] Ibid., §7147.

[9] Ibid.

[10] Cf. Ingrid Riedel, *Formen. Kreis, Kreuz, Dreieck, Quadrat, Spirale,* Kreuz, Stuttgart 1985, 89ff.

[11] Cf. Jung, *CW* 9;1, § 710.

[12] Jaak Panksepp and LucyBiven, *The Archaeology of Mind. Neuroevolutionary Origins of Human Emotions.* New York W.W. Norton, 2012, 283 ff.

[13] Jung, CW 9:1, §16.

[14] Cf. ibid. § 622

[15] Report on the German Seminar by Dr. C.G. Jung, compiled by Olga von Koenig.Fachsenfeld. Private print, Stuttgart 1931.

[16] Cf. ibid., 87ff.

[17Cf.] Verena Kast, *Imagination. Zugänge zu inneren Ressourcen finden.* Completely revised new edition, Patmos, Ostfildern, 2012.

[18] Cf. Jung, *CW* 9:1, § 676.

"But why do I encourage patients... to express themselves by means of brush, pencil, or pen at all?"

—C.G. JUNG

Ruth Ammann

Many texts in C.G. JUNG's writings bear witness to the importance he attached to painting and drawing in the framework of Analytical Therapy. Still, the text below was of such interest and preoccupation to me that I decided to select it as the main theme for this chapter.

In "The Aims of Psychotherapy," *Collected Works*, Vol. 16, Jung writes:

> But why do I encourage patients, when they arrive at a certain stage in their development, to express themselves by means of brush, pencil, or pen at all? [...] Here again my prime purpose is to produce an effect. In the state of psychological childhood described above, the patient remains passive. But now, he begins to play an active part. To start off with, he puts down on paper what he has passively seen, thereby turning it into a deliberate act. He not only talks about it, he is actually doing something about it. Psychologically speaking, it makes a vast difference whether a man has an interesting conversation with his doctor two or three times a week, the results of which are left hanging in mid air, or whether he has to struggle for hours with refractory brush and colors, only to produce in the end something which, taken at its face value, is perfectly senseless. If it were really senseless to him, the effort to paint it would be so repugnant that he could scarcely be brought to perform this exercise a second time.[1]

Jung remarks that his prime purpose is to produce an effect. Does he refer to an intellectual or an emotional effect, or perhaps to a sensual, physical one? Or does he refer to a sensual-emotional effect that might result in a psychological insight? It is probably all of that, as painting and drawing are very sensual activities with an impact on the body, as well as the soul and the psyche.

What happens then if someone is painting? Let me attempt to comprehensibly describe what I myself experience when I'm painting: Thoughts, feelings, and pictures are floating inside of us, like a picturesque state of being that flows and condenses in connection with the very nature of color by means of exploratory movements of the hand and paintbrush. Each color has its own attributes, own vibration, emotional charisma and specific symbolism. The entire process of drawing and painting is a somewhat flowing, searching and groping activity, undecided up to the very moment the paint starts to dry, eventually taking its solid shape. Then, a new process sets in: the radiant power of the newly blended color rebounds on both body and soul, triggering new thoughts and emotions. It is a unique process from flowing to shaped and back to flowing energy. This formative process has an enormous holistic impact on humans.

Let us return to a passage in the quote from "The Aims of Psychotherapy":

> Psychologically speaking, it makes a vast difference whether a man has an interesting conversation with his doctor two or three times a week, the results of which are left hanging in midair, or whether he has to struggle for hours with refractory brush and colors...

This phrase will probably trigger the same question in each reader: "Does Jung put drawing and painting above the conversation, even above the verbal exploration of dreams?" This seems to be the case here.

I have been pondering over this sentence for quite a while. It may be understood in the way that talking comes easy to us, sometimes "it" simply talks. Transforming our yet unorganized inner pictures into a visual, palpable and also meaningful shape, however, demands great artistic endeavor. I have also traced this sentence on a physical level, as a bodily experience, and a quote from Johann Wolfgang von Goethe's work "The Theory of Colors"2 came to mind. Goethe was not only a great poet, he was also a researcher. In his work on the theory of colors, he describes the experience in which looking at colors equals "transforming what you see into what you feel." He explains that "the sharpest of all senses, vision, shall dissolve in the dullest, the tactile sense, to make it more conceivable to us." Color would only exist "insofar as it may become palpable."[3] What does that mean? In my understanding, we need to transition from seeing to groping, from seeing to palpation and feeling with our hands or our entire bodies. We do know that vision is the sharpest of all human senses, the most commonly used and best developed. Seeing, however, also leads to quick assumptions about objects.

There is a connection between the perception of an object and the rapid intellectual analysis of what we have seen. Merely "seeing" an object, for example a picture, may therefore lure us into superficiality. We are only too quick in assuming that we have understood a painting. In order to dive deeper and explore the background of colors and shapes, we need the tactile sense, which, however, is much less sharpened and clear. It is also slower, carefully searching. Even if our hands are extremely sensitive organs, palpitation is more difficult to translate into words, particularly into intellectual terms and concepts. We do not only feel with our hands, but with our entire bodies, and transform what we have felt into thoughts, emotions and intuitions. I reckon that even intuition is a kind of tactile sense. With a view to experiencing paintings, Goethe asks us to not only see with the intellectual eye, but with the entire body, to sense and feel with all available senses and physiological functions.

Perhaps Jung intended to express something similar by asking: "But why do I encourage patients to express themselves by means of brush, pencil or pen at all? Here again my prime purpose is to produce an effect." He wanted his patients to struggle with objectively unfamiliar materials and their subjective, yet unconscious aspects. He wanted them to be touched and shaken by an experience that would shift the center of gravity of their personality.

I would like to illustrate the way in which Jung's patients have complied with his request for drawing and painting with the example of several pictures painted by a roughly 50-year-old woman. I am going to call her "A." The picture series in the Archive are normally referenced with only very short comments or no comments at all. The one illustrated here is therefore a "windfall" for our Archive, as A has painted approximately 90 pictures over the course of two years and added very personal explanatory notes on the back. The texts are spontaneous, erratic, and not always easy for today's readers to understand. A addresses Jung with "you" – and we do not know whether she had an inner figure in the shape of Jung in mind or in fact Jung himself as the analyst.

The series is archived under "Case 039."[4] A described dreams, emotions, and fantasies that inspired her to paint, or vice versa – which emerged from her paintings. Some sequences are genuine Active Imaginations in the way Jung has formulated them,[5] meaning that one picture develops out of the other in the process of imagination. In the same way, explanatory notes continuously develop out of preceding ones.

Of particular interest are the many passages in which A addresses Jung directly as her analyst, and he also talks to her. This inner dialogue extended over the entire course of the analysis. In many passages, strong and oftentimes very erotically charged transference fantasies become visible and tangible. We do not know to what extent this dialogue has merely sprung from A's fantasies or the actual conversations with Jung. The texts clearly show a mixture of both. (What we do know is that Jung discussed not only his own pictures, but that of his patients with them. Many pictures in the Archive painted by Jung's patients bear a resemblance to his own). In any case, A's pictures and texts enable us to slowly approach the intense and intimate process of Analytical Therapy.

In the explanatory notes to her first colored picture (not shown here), A described her struggle to indulge in the painting process:

> *Autumn 1927. Through the entire fall, it seemed rather impossible to me to draw or paint out of imagination. I was almost paralyzed. The first seven attempts were desperate endeavors against my inclination and meant almost nothing to me. The drawings look like the little pictures I painted as a twelve-year-old. While those were realistic attempts, these here are simply decorative efforts.*

The text shows A's difficulties with painting.

Feelings of rejection and doubts in one's own skills are generally experienced by patients when we ask them to paint their inner Pictures. During Jung's time and even today, they struggle to devote themselves to painting.

In the next picture (039 BMAH) and the accompanying text, A already revealed quite a lot. She was around 50 years old, fearful, but courageous enough to climb a steep staircase without handrails. We also recognize that she was a meticulous, patient painter. I am impressed by the nuanced, solid, and masculinely structured depiction of the wall and the temple, in contrast to the soft, flowing and rather feminine colors in the background. A is right in the middle of the picture, at the crossing point of these opposites so to say, climbing the steep wall leading to the temple.

Text on the reverse of picture 039 BMAH:

I dreamt about climbing a long and rather narrow staircase. Large cuboids of crumbling stone – nothing to hold on to – fear of falling down. Halfway, referring to age 50, I stop. I then continue climbing up the stairs. Right at the top is the entrance to a temple in which a high priest is waiting to welcome me.

In terms of color and form, the subsequent picture (039 BMAI) is very strong, static and bold. An intense radiance emanates from the densely layered paint, with the two shades of red and the flaming orange sword gleaming towards us. Against the strong green floor and the stark blue background, the character seems rather dignified to me, sacred,

039 BMAH · Anonymous, untitled, text on the reverse, 17 January 1928. Gouache on paper, 29 x 23 cm. Picture Archive of the C.G. Jung Institute Zürich-Küsnacht

also masculine, but with the addition of a feminine touch. The intense eyes, the sword and the colors are truly fascinating. From which subconscious depths did the slim woman on the wall draw the strength to paint this picture? Perhaps from her father, who in fact handed the sword to her?

Text on the reverse of picture 039 BMAI:

As I am unable to imagine something priestly that could impress or console me, this phallic, scarlet red figure is the best I can create. It now holds aloft something that I originally intended to paint as a flaming sword, but that now resembles a sword that my father brought with him from Africa.

039 BMAI
19 January 1928

039 BMAK
21 January 1928

039 BMAL
22 January 1928

All: Anonymous, untitled, text on reverse. Gouache on paper, 29 x 23 cm
Picture Archive of the C.G. Jung Institute Zürich-Küsnacht

Jung commented on the picture with the tulip (039 BMAK).[6] Following my own feelings and thoughts, however, I see an attempt to hold together and endure the very strong emotion that the red figure with the sword must have evoked in her - similar to the following, very aesthetic picture with the kingfisher (039 BMAL).

Text on the reverse of picture 039 BMAK:

You suggested that I paint a picture of what I would see next – upon entering the temple. With the crazy thought that this might be heaven. I believe a circle is the only way to illustrate this. I place the growing flower in the center as a symbol for creation and attainment.

Text on the reverse of picture 039 BMAL:

Still with the lingering thought of illustrating heaven, attainment, or the greatest possible fulfillment, I am painting this picture of the kingfisher that points north, east, south and west.

A painted these two pictures (039 BMAK and 039 BMAL) within a period of six days, followed by another four simpler, more abstract ones (039 BMAM, 039 BMAN, 039 BMAO, and 039 BMAP).

All of them show a strong centralizing spatial orientation. Circles and squares are holding the psychical energy together, possibly alluding to the fact that A was in danger of becoming overwhelmed by still unconscious, undifferentiated, and probably excessive fantasies, induced by the Pictures of heaven, the temple, and the priest. My guess is that A painted these centralizing pictures

039 BMAH · Anonymous, untitled, text on the reverse, 17 January 1928
Gouache on paper, 29 x 23 cm
Picture Archive of the C.G. Jung Institute Zürich-Küsnacht

039 BMAI · Anonymous, untitled, text on the reverse, 19 January 1928
Gouache on paper, 29 x 23 cm
Picture Archive of the C.G. Jung Institute Zürich-Küsnacht

039 BMAK · Anonymous, untitled, text on reverse, 21 January 1928
Gouache on paper, 29 x 23 cm
Picture Archive of the C.G. Jung Institute Zürich-Küsnacht

039 BMAL · Anonymous, untitled, text on the reverse, 22 January 1928
Gouache on paper, 29 x 23 cm
Picture Archive of the C.G. Jung Institute Zürich, Küsnacht

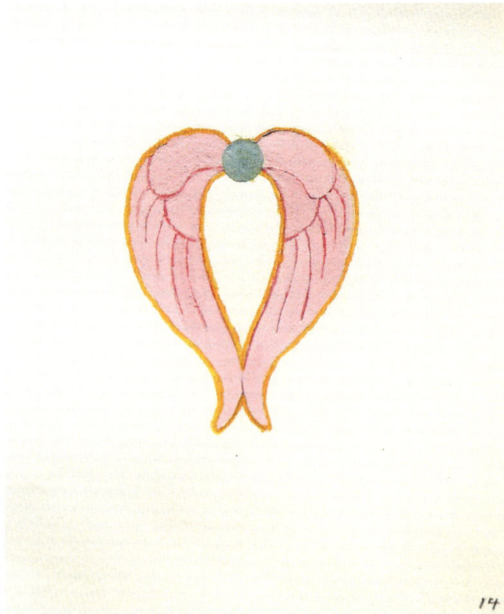

Upper Row, Left: **039 BMAM**, 23 January 1928
Upper Row, Right: **039 BMAN**, 24 January 1928
Lower Row, Left: **039 BMAO**, 24 January 1928
Lower Row, Right: **039 BMAP**, 25 January 1928
Above and next page: Gouache on paper, 29 x 23 cm
Picture Archive of the C.G. Jung Institute Zürich-Küsnacht

039 BMAQ Anonymous, untitled, text on reverse, 27 January 1928.

039 BMAR · Anonymous, untitled, text on reverse, 29 January 1928

out of instinct: the paintbrush provided the shapes that corresponded to her strong emotions, thus leading her back to her own center. The small pictures do not carry any explanatory notes, suggesting that words were not needed here.

Then, Jung seemed to have mentioned that it was too early to "climb up to heaven" (039 BMAQ), A would have to "concern herself with the mysteries" first. I assume that he referred to the Demeter Mysteries, an induction into the mystery of the feminine.[7]

In my own words, I would say that each temple or tower needs a solid foundation in the ground. In the same way, each development of the spirit or aspiring intellect needs a solid foundation in the body, the feminine and the emotional realm. The higher the temple above, the deeper the foundation must be anchored in the ground. A therefore needed to orientate herself "downwards", towards her own femininity.

The picture depicting a cross-section of a sprouting wheat grain with chaff is beautiful (039 BMAQ). Its colors are delicately nuanced with lively inner shapes, but held by two squares. The green sprout inside the grain resembles the shape of the red figure's sword.

The two blue squares, offset against each other by 45°, form an octagon, which is the very shape that transcends the square as a symbol of the earth to the circle, symbolizing heaven. In Christianity, the octagon is found in baptisteries as a shape for recommencement and resurrection. Was A aware of this profound symbolism in her picture?

Text on the reverse of picture 039 BMAQ:

You said it was still too early for heaven – I try to paint the growth of a wheat grain.

The next picture (039 BMAR) does not have

039 BMAQ · Anonymous, untitled, text on reverse, 27 January 1928
Gouache on paper, 29 x 23 cm
Picture Archive of the C.G. Jung Institute Zürich-Küsnacht

039 BMAR · Anonymous, untitled, text on reverse, 29 January 1928
Gouache on paper, 29 x 23 cm
Picture Archive of the C.G. Jung Institute Zürich-Küsnacht

039 BMAS · Anonymous, untitled, text on reverse, 30 January 1928
Gouache on paper, 29 x 23 cm
Picture Archive of the C.G. Jung Institute Zürich-Küsnacht

039 BMAT · Anonymous, untitled, text on reverse, 2 February 1928
Gouache on paper, 29 x 23 cm
Picture Archive of the C.G. Jung Institute Zürich-Küsnacht

any words and does not need any either. I dare mention, though, that this picture, like many other of A's works, alludes to the time in which she lived. It contains strong Art Deco elements, an art form that was close to Art Nouveau and in fashion around 1920 to 1940.

The following picture (039 BMAS) and its text speak for themselves, too. Just look at the soft, sensual shapes and colors!

Text on the reverse of picture 039 BMAS:

This is an illustration of how I start to feel –female depths, very sexual, breaking open.

A couple of days later, however, the situation had changed. I assume that the awakening femininity and sexuality strongly invigorated A's fantasies about her analyst. This does not come as a surprise, since Jung was a little over 50 years old at the time and certainly a very handsome man who attracted many projections. Nevertheless, I dare say that in the explanatory notes of picture 039 BMAT below, not Jung himself is cited, but A's "inner" Jung.

Text on the reverse of picture 039 BMAT:

You tell me that I should go deeper into the temple. First, there is a long corridor with

flickering lights, taking on the symbolic shapes I painted. But suddenly, I see, flickering but clearly, a winding snake, brown with dark spots. My heart, terrified, is pounding so hard that I cannot go any further and I paint this picture. I try mightily to paint the egg clearly.

Contemplating the stylized apple tree and the snake, the temptation in paradise naturally comes to mind. Looking at the text, though, it is quite obvious that A had traced her imaginations and was terrified by the appearance of the snake to such an extent that she had to paint this picture in order to maintain the sexual emotion. In this picture, the snake is still faceless.

In the next picture (039 BMAU), however, it shows its face. It appears to be frightening, eerie, but somehow also ambiguous, unpleasant. A referred to the snake as male. After contemplating it for a while, it seems to be male and female to me, though; the dangerous face is male, the body is female.

Behind the snake, we see a transparent, ghost-like being with its hands crossed in front of its chest, as if it had to protect itself/himself/herself from the enormous snake energy.

Text on the reverse of picture 039 BMAU:

A corridor leads to a stone staircase, very steep. I almost fall. At the end, there is a nice big room, high, dark at the sides. You are standing in the light, softly saying: "See? This is all there is." I understand that you are trying to encourage me in a

039 BMAU · Anonymous, untitled, text on reverse, 3 February 1928
Gouache on paper, 29 x 23 cm
Picture Archive of the C.G. Jung Institute Zürich-Küsnacht

very friendly way, but also that I have to go all by myself – so I continue walking towards the shadow, where I expect to find the snake. High up on the wall, there is a picture, a fresco of a kind of supernatural figure. Below, I see the snake, huge and dreadful, with yellow spots, winding itself and lifting its head. I approach him ["Him" indicates that the snake is male -RA], *terrified, I have to touch him. I suddenly realize that I am sexually very aroused. I want to proceed, but there is darkness all around me. Alone in this horror. Suddenly, a door opens towards a loggia flooded with light,*

039 BMAS · Anonymous, untitled, text on reverse 30 January 1928
Gouache on paper, 29 x 23 cm
Picture Archive of the C.G. Jung Institute Zürich-Küsnacht

039 BMAT · Anonymous, untitled, text on reverse 2 February 1928
Gouache on paper, 29 x 23 cm
Picture Archive of the C.G. Jung Institute Zürich-Küsnacht

039 BMAU · Anonymous, untitled, text on reverse, 3 February 1928
Gouache on paper, 29 x 23 cm
Picture Archive of the C.G. Jung Institute Zürich-Küsnacht

and at its end, but coming towards me, a beautiful baby – like a little renaissance angel. And there are renaissance decorations in the loggia, on the columns and above. I am touched and emotional, but all of a sudden, I realize that this is probably only a Freudian wish-fulfillment dream and I feel relegated to reality.

Going back to the initial quote by Jung, "But why do I encourage patients to express themselves by means of brush, pencil, or pen at all? Here again my prime purpose is to produce an effect", we can clearly see the emotional and physical impact that the Pictures surfacing from the unconscious in A's pictures have on her. In a merely therapeutic conversation, emotions would have been triggered, but never to such an enormous extent, intensified by colors and shapes. What we can also see is that Active Imagination as a method, or allowing inner Pictures to emerge and painting them, is not a harmless process. Physical-mental forces are being unleashed – like those in the picture of the snake – that cannot be maintained and transformed on one's own. It is not about mental energies alone, it is also about holistic, physical ones. A, too, needed help from her doctor and analyst. The text reveals her reaction at the time of writing: she needed to debilitate the horror, so she had to downplay her feelings, depreciating them as "only Freudian wish-fulfillment thinking" in order to be able to endure them.

Let us return once more to the picture with the apple tree and the snake (009 BMAT).

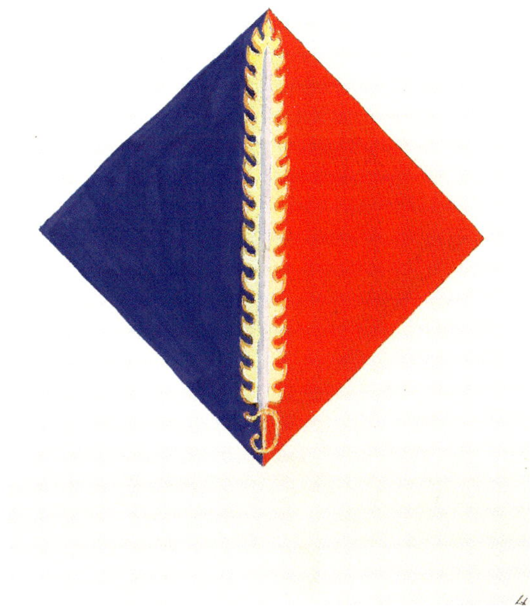

039 BMBU · Anonymous, untitled, text on reverse, 24 March 1928
Gouache on paper, 29 x 23 cm
Picture Archive of the C.G. Jung Institute Zürich-Küsnacht

While painting, A attached great importance to the egg at the foot of the tree. It was extremely important to her as it contains – probably as yet unconsciously – the seed of her new personality, or her male and her female-motherly side. In 22 subsequent paintings, one each day, a baby develops out of the egg, a small boy, then a man and her relationship as a woman to these inner figures.

Showing these pictures here would go beyond the scope of this book, but interested readers are invited to study the entire series in the Picture Archive.

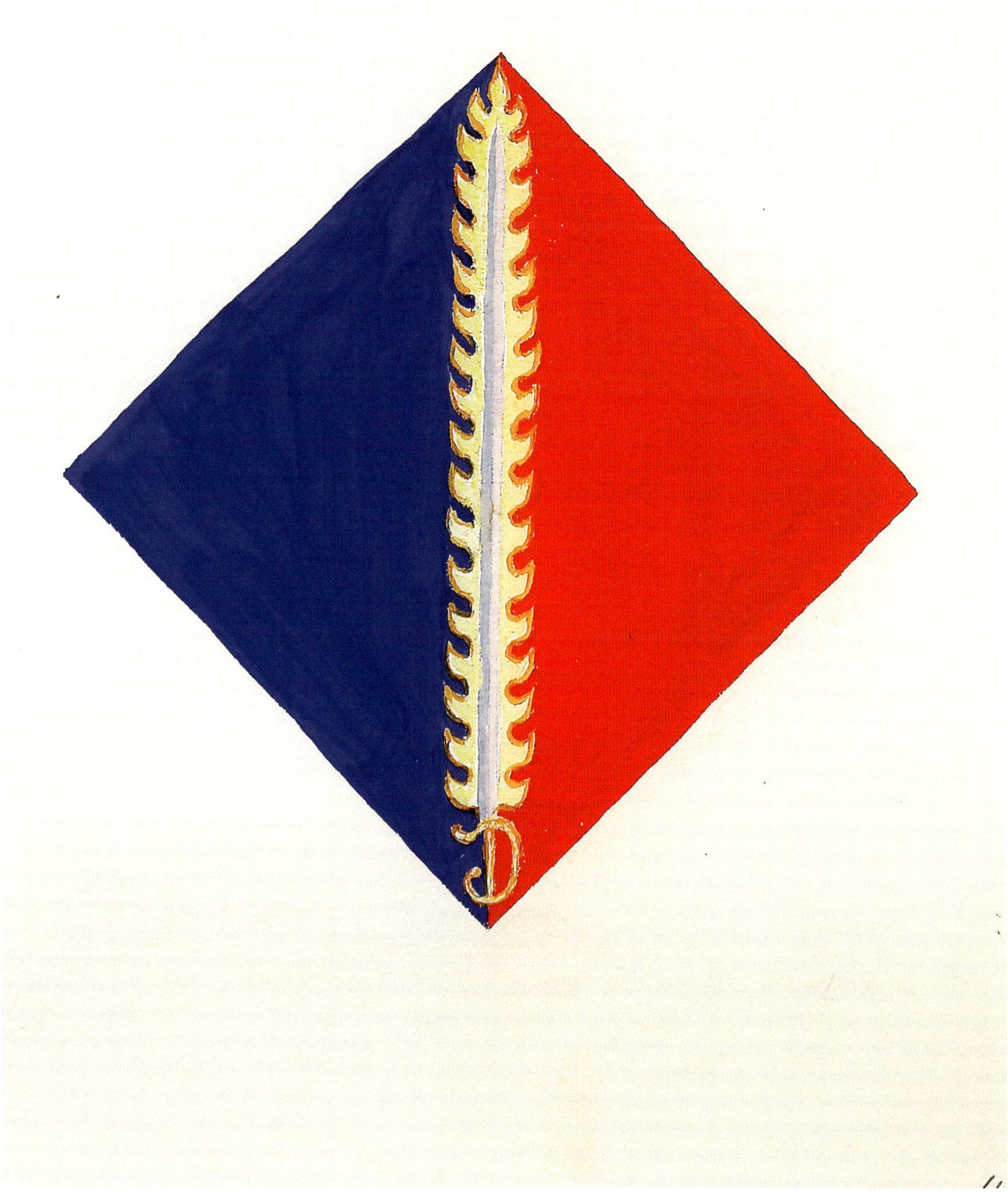

039 BMBU · Anonymous, untitled, text on reverse, 24 March 1928
Gouache on paper, 29 x 23 cm.
Picture Archive of the C.G. Jung Institute Zürich-Küsnacht

I am now going to jump from 3 February to 23 March 1928, to picture BMBU.

Again, A talked to her analyst.

Text on the reverse of 039 BMBU:

But when I enter the house again, you are not there. The wind is moving the curtains. Everything is empty and restless. Confused and miserable, I feel you might have gone into the temple downstairs. I ask myself why men like temples more than they like houses. I stop here and follow you. The red columns remind me of the Temple of Heaven. Shyly, I enter. The large room in which I saw you is empty. On the left side, a door is hidden behind a curtain. I walk through another large room, a very gloomy, dark red place. I see a huge red sofa And right opposite the door, there is a sword, illuminated in a stage-like manner. There is also a huge globe, swinging in a frame that is higher than the middle. I feel very much left alone and I assume it is this kind of place where Isadora would have liked to dance, but I didn't like it. From the covered wall behind the sword, a small white kitten suddenly appears. It has deep blue eyes and looks up to me, then turns around and disappears behind the sword again. There seems to be a corridor. I follow it and find another, very dark room, but to my unspeakable relief, I see your outstretched hand in your blue coat sleeve. I seize it and you drag me into the room and sit down beside me. I feel completely cocooned and safe and happy and then, you point towards a door at the other end, where a shimmering iridescent light appears. I see a blue building like the Temple of Heaven. I picture it the way it really is and see you standing in a circle, open towards heaven, where the ruler used to kneel.

But everything is false. The painting of the sword signifies strongly divided opposites. I am too simple. Totally confused and desperate. I have been sent on holidays for months. Ms. Wolff is nice and sees me a couple of times in order to dampen the shock.

Obviously, A was ripped out of her imagination after Jung had left, presumably having retreated into his tower in Bollingen to go on vacation or to study. A was confronted with reality, completely confused and desperate. Her disappointment about Jung "leaving" her led to her negative judgment about the picture and herself. As a matter of fact, the sword separates the opposites of blue and red, of active and passive, male and female. The red color jumps at us, while the blue color retreats. Many opposing aspects of red and blue are divided by the sword – or united. The jagged sword, in a very trivial way, also looks like a uniting zipper to me. As we can read in the text, Toni Wolff jumped in to connect the disrupted relationship to Jung in the real world.

Text on the reverse of 039 BMCI (next page):

I envision a gift of fruit in an Indian bowl. It leads me to the idea to visit you in your

039 BMCI · Anonymous, untitled, text on reverse, 15 June 1928
Gouache on paper, 29 x 23 cm
Picture Archive of the C.G. Jung Institute Zürich-Küsnacht

tower in the countryside, it makes me truly happy.

Between March and October, A painted numerous pictures and wrote short texts, but without addressing Jung. Only once did she have a fantasy which she depicted in picture 039 BMCI, which is somewhat touching in its almost naïve simplicity.

There may certainly be a correlation with picture 039 BMAT, where the snake is winding itself up the apple tree, and the apples could be considered as erotic symbols. They are also round, tempting, very sensual. But this gesture of presenting a simple bowl of apples, the primordial fruit of our country, to one's analyst is so mundane, so touchingly remote from temples, heaven, huge projections and exceeded transference Pictures, that I start to develop a warm and friendly feeling for A's picture. I imagine that Toni Wolff, the "substitute", appealed to and developed a new and down-to-earth side in A.

Text on the reverse of BMED:

Out of depression and confusion, the blue terror is winding up. I feel that this might be my archaic thinking. You note that he obviously cannot endure the light of day, as he seems to scurry back.

After having been on holidays for three months herself, without pictures and texts, A started her second year of analysis in October 1928. I have selected yet another picture (039 BMED) from

039 BMED · Anonymous, untitled, text on reverse, 26 March 1929
Gouache on paper, 29 x 23 cm
Picture Archive of the C.G. Jung Institute Zürich-Küsnacht

April 1928, the 89th in the series, one of the last ones.

The explanatory notes are gloomy. Still, knowing about the entire picture and text series, I venture to offer a less gloomy interpretation of the work.

It is my favorite among A's pictures, radiating an unbelievable power. The densely applied paint covers the entire sheet, not a single white stripe is left out. We see the royal blue "monster" with its light green spine, winding itself out of the dark left bottom corner up towards the sun, not simply back into darkness, but head-on towards the observer, establishing contact with us. Its eyes are like headlights – what are they trying to tell us?

039 BMED · Anonymous, untitled, text on reverse, 26 March 1929
Gouache on paper, 29 x 23 cm
Picture Archive of the C.G. Jung Institute Zürich-Küsnacht

039 BMEK · Anonymous, untitled, text on reverse, 16 June 1929
Gouache on paper, 29 x 23 cm
Picture Archive of the C.G. Jung Institute Zürich-Küsnacht

Compared to the 12th picture (039 BMAI), where bright red and blue are separated (or united) by the sword, the colors have now changed. The body of the creature is still blue, but the masculine, active, also aggressive red has become more differentiated and can be found in the lighter, upper part of the picture. A blend of some light red and yellow creates a bright, radiant orange that reminds us of light and day. The bottom part of the picture is heavy, a combination of dark red and blue turns into dark purple, which in turn is reminiscent of earth, darkness and night. There are strong opposites in the picture: above and below, light and heavy, bright orange and dark purple, day and night.

In the bottom left corner, there is a dark circle, shaped by the monster's tail – and another circle in bright orange in the upper right corner, the sun. It is safe to say that the strong tension between the circles represents the dark unconscious and the luminous conscious mind.

The monster is visibly more entangled in the dark underworld, but look at the vigor with which it still grabs some light from the upper world! This process seems to keep repeating itself, as the blue body is almost shaped like an eternity symbol. We are even able to trace this movement with our hands!

Yet, there is still more to see: The monster's head, another circle, connects the dark circle in the bottom left with the sun circle in the upper right corner; it is the Third, emerging from the tension between the unconscious and the conscious, bearing the unification of opposites, the new, the unexpected. I picture the blue monster to say: "I am the transcendent function that connects conscious and unconscious content." Jung notes that "there is nothing mysterious or metaphysical about the term 'transcendent function' […].,"[8] which certainly holds true for the function itself, but not for anything that emerges from it: Is there anything more mystical than a picture that has emerged as something new from the unification of conscious and unconscious content? I don't think so. Both A's picture series and the many other series in the Picture Archive are secrets that were painted and drawn with great diligence and dedication, created by the mysterious connection of the conscious and unconscious mind. They still have an impact on us today that we will not forget.

The "secret" is unveiled, not entirely, but to some extent, in the last picture of the series, dated 16 June 1929 (picture 039 BMEK). An interpretation seems to be impossible, but I'd like to carefully approach the impact that it has on us.

A soft, elegant shape – a funnel, a flower, a trumpet flower? – is growing out of the water. It seems to nourish itself from the moist, the floating. It is red, but it is a soft, slightly orange red, feminine, sensual. The trumpet, too, feels sensual, feminine, reminiscent of the early illustration of female sexuality. Countless winged creatures are emerging from its inside, wafting away, we can almost see and feel them fluttering. They are bright, shining, playful. Are these ideas? Mind games? Dreams? Fantasies? Projections? Projects? We do not know. We can only see that they are born out of soft, feminine depth, which in turn nourishes itself from the water. A remarked that most of the butterfly creatures are going to die, decay, and only one will – perhaps – survive. Is it the uppermost butterfly? It seems to fly away, gleaming like a star.

We do not know where it will descend. This remains a secret even after almost a hundred pictures! And still, although the background of A's life is unknown to us, we were able to cast a deep glance into the colors, shapes and words of her soul. She has given us a lot. We do not have to understand, but the content is certainly perceptible and palpable. In this way, A is leaving a trace in our memories.

Text on the reverse of 039 BMEK:

This was created out of a surging feeling that expressed itself in these shapes and colors. But the butterflies were suggested by you, mentioning Maeterlinck's "La vie des Termites" and the enormous waste at their annual sacrifice. After a long period of an unbelievably economical and self-sustaining life, the day comes when they emerge, buzzing, thousands of small winged creatures that are mainly going to die – perhaps one survives.

039 BMEK · Anonymous, untitled, text on reverse
16 June 1929. Gouache on paper, 29 x 23 cm
Picture Archive of the C.G. Jung Institute Zürich-Küsnacht

Notes

1 Jung, "The Aims of Psychotherapy" (1926) § 105 f.

2 Goethe, *Zur Farbenlehre* (1810), 111.

3 Translated by the author from the original.

4 Case 039, Picture Archive of the C.G. Jung Institute Zürich / Küsnacht.

5 Jung, To Mr. O., letter of 2 May 1947, in: *Encountering: Jung on Active Imagination,* 164.

6 Jung, "Concerning Mandala Symbolism," Figure 11, § 661.

7 Demeter Mysteries: The Mysteries of Eleusis.

8 Cf. Jung, "The Transcendent Function," § 131

References

Case 039 Picture Archive of the C.G. Jung Institute Zürich-Küsnacht.

Demeter Mysteries: The Mysteries of Eleusis.

Goethe, Johann Wolfgang von: *Zur Farbenlehre* (1810). WA Abt. II, Bd. 3, 111.

Jung, C.G.: The Transcendent Function, *Collected Works* (CW), Vol. 8: *The Structure and Dynamics of the Psyche.* Bollingen Series XX, Princeton University Press, Princeton NJ, 1969. Figure 11, § 131.

—— The Aims of Psychotherapy (1926). In: CW 16: *The Practice of Psychotherapy. Essays on the Psychology of the Transference and Other Subjects.* Bollingen Series XX. Princeton, NJ: Princeton University Press, 1966. §§ 105 f.

—— To Mr. O., letter of 2 May 1947, in: *Encountering: Jung on Active Imagination,* Edited and with an Introduction by Joan Chodorow. Princeton, NJ: Princeton University Press, Princeton NJ, 1997, 164.

—— Concerning Mandala Symbolism. In: CW 9/I: *The Archetypes and the Collective Unconscious.* Bollingen Series XX. Princeton, NJ: Princeton University Press, 1969. Figure 11, § 661.

Apocolyptic Times

A PICTURE SERIES FROM THE SECOND WORLD WAR

Ingrid Riedel

The Picture Series – General Information

THE SERIES COMPRISES A total of 28 pictures, twelve of which have been exhibited, and is registered today under Code 041 (BO) in the Picture Archive of the C.G. Jung Institute in Zürich. The fact that Jung originally kept this picture series in his own collection suggests that a therapeutic contact existed between him and the person who painted these pictures, and that they discussed them, not least to work through the traumatic war experiences they contain. Who was this individual?

The personal context of the pictures is limited to the hand-written annotations attached to them. Judging, among other things, from several characteristics in the writing style typical for a certain generation, the painter was probably a roughly 40-year-old German woman who lived through the war, and especially the bombardments, in one of the major German cities. The pictures are dated 1939 to 1945, but there are also some from 1947, which suggests that several were created immediately after, but others probably still during the war. Maybe the painter was seeing Jung directly after the war for analysis. The pictures are well structured. In terms of painting technique, poster paint is thickly applied onto thin board, which contributes to the inner significance of the series becoming immediately tangible. To date, the pictures have not been published. They were, however, displayed at the Zum Höchhuus Gallery in Küsnacht in 1998 on the occasion of the 50-year anniversary of the C.G. Jung Institute Zürich. Back then, Kathrin Asper provided psychological commentaries on the series which proved invaluable to me.

Apocalyptic Times

"The storm over Germany is about to break loose! 1939. Demons of fire – nurtured by blood", is the picture caption that the painter herself wrote on the back of the respective pictures (041 BOAB). "Apocalyptic Times" is the title of this picture that I chose as the first to be depicted here, although it was created in the middle of the series – it seems to be a vision of what was to come. She noted the year 1939, which marked the beginning of World War II with Hitler's Germany attacking the neighboring countries, starting with Poland. The painter experienced the impact of these attacks - the Allied bombardments of German cities - as a

041 BOAB · "Apocalyptic times: The Storm over Germany is about to break loose! 1939
Demons of fire – nurtured by blood"
Anonymous, 1939, gouache on thin board, 24.7 x 17.4 cm
Picture Archive of the C.G. Jung Institute Zürich-Küsnacht

civilian in a major German city. "Demons of fire" broke loose, "nurtured by blood", the blood of the hundreds of thousands of people who perished in these bombardments.

She experienced the air raids as something supernatural. "Demons of fire" break forth. The violence emanates from the demon in the top left quadrant of the picture – in which, as experience shows, superordinate and fateful symbols oftentimes appear – and diagonally crosses the picture towards the right-hand bottom corner, almost aiming at the symbolical space of security (as known in art therapy suggested by Jolande Jacobi). The attack targets the symbolic space of security - also in the painter herself. The composition of this picture seems to be a visionary compression of what was happening, the air raids between 1942 and 1945.

The flaming demon is sent down into the pictorial space "from heaven", a place that is usually associated with the good, but here, it turns into a dark horizon of fate. The scales on its back and legs allude to a dragon-like creature whose curved tail eventually reaches back down into the earth from which it has ascended. A huge fire flares up from the same crater the demon has risen from, almost like a sacrificial fire.

The dragon figure dominates the picture, painted in a hot red. The fire itself, permeated by smoke, radiates a cooler shade of red than that of the dragon, a red tone, almost bleeding into purple. This fire, again, is blazing from the earth high up into the sky. Contemplating it, one is almost tempted to think of the "burning bush", in which case, however, the fire would have an entirely different quality. Not an ominous dragon, but a symbolic idea - which is by no means far-fetched, given the deeply religious painter of this series as whom she was going to reveal herself later on.

The dragon in the picture leaves traces of energy, whose tips are swinging to the left like loopings, before turning back and down again towards the bottom right, eventually taking the concrete shape of airplanes, spraying out their explosive load in fiery colors while passing through the purple blaze, before finally targeting the lower region on the right-hand side of the painting. As already mentioned, this side of the picture is the symbolic space particularly associated with a sense of safety and security, of being at home in a motherly environment. So this is where the attack is aimed at in the painter's life. Creating this picture probably became emotionally necessary after she had been wounded in this area. As the personal context is lacking, the interpretation is limited to the rather objective, collective symbolism of a war of annihilation that destroys the security of what we call home or homeland. On the other hand, it creates some relevance for similar happenings in today's world, such as the bombardments of cities in the Near and Middle East, which have left millions of people homeless.

In this composition, the crater or well at the bottom of the picture seems strange to me. Bursting open from the grayish-blue and black mounds, it looks as if both the fire-spitting dragon and the sacrificial fire are rising from it at the same time. The bomber squadrons of the former are spattering down like burning arrows onto the hostile city, from heaven, in a revenging God-like manner. The latter might symbolize the burning bush in which Moses saw God's presence, calling on him to lead the people out of servitude. Hatred, violence and destruction against humans on the one hand, reverence and the will of liberation and sacrifice on the other: both stem from the same deep source - ambivalent human nature. Both aspects must have agitated and distressed the painter of this picture series, probably leaving her traumatized.

Dead Street

The painter's annotations on the back of the picture read: "Dead Street. Dream at the beginning of the war, December 1939" (041 BOAC). As the caption shows, the picture obviously relates to a dream that the women had at the beginning of World War II, still before the anticipated events had actually taken place, and that she was unable to forget; she must have created this picture either immediately at the time of the dream or after the war so as to remember it.

We can see the street shooting up steeply from the bottom left to the upper right part of the painting, which is spatially symbolic for the direction leading into the future. Broad, heavy black tempera brush strokes, also alternating with red-black-red ones, introduce shades of tension and destruction. Ruins of houses line both sides of the road, with their broken facades reaching high up into the sky and black beams protruding into the street. At the bottom right – the symbolic space for safety and security – stones come hailing down from the destroyed houses right in the front of the picture, painted as black lumps against a brown background. At the far right, a towering ruin of a five- or multi-story building appears in blackish-blue, with black empty windows. It could well be the house of the painter, even her childhood home, as it is located in the symbolic quadrant of motherly security, at the bottom right. The pain of having lost a home symbolizes itself in this picture and might even have caused its creation. In the foreboding dream that she has painted here, everything is already destroyed. The city is dead, not a single soul in sight. The overarching red sky is not the rising sun, but the glow of fire.

Once a premonition, this dream has now turned into a memory. I, too, wandered through these cities in my childhood. Dreading the strong wind and avoiding the streets, we had to be careful not to get hit by crumbling ruins. This context reminds us of C.G. Jung's recurring dream of a cold coming in from outer space, which he dreamt three times, in April, May and June 1914. Before the outbreak of World War I, he also understood this to be a premonition.[1]

041 BOAC · "DEAD STREET. DREAM AT THE BEGINNING OF THE WAR"
Anonymous, 1939, gouache on thin board, 24.7 x 17.4 cm
Picture Archive of the C.G. Jung Institute Zürich-Küsnacht

War and Death

As the picture caption mentions the entire period from 1939 to 1945 (041 BOAF), it seems obvious that it was created after this period, which for the woman concerned is themed "War:Death." An enormous storm, known to be caused by large fires, breaks forth from the right side of the picture, the outside world. It enters the pictorial environment, where a human being – the helmet indicates that he is a soldier – is left without defense. The tree's stem still withstands the storm, but has already lost its crown. The soldier is stretching out his arms, imploringly, and is thrown back, about to fall, like the rifle that has already slipped from his hands. His gesture is touching, he is almost kneeling down, beseeching, yet already without hope. Behind his back and under the roots of the tree, there is still a small patch of light, but no chance to withstand the forces of the black-red firestorm.

These firestorms, unleashed by burning city quarters, could be observed with sheer horror in cities like Munich, Dresden and in my hometown, the industrial city of Schweinfurt. Once drawn into these forces, humans were lost. The man with the helmet is a symbol for everyone affected by war, not only civilians in the cities. He could also be reminiscent of the "unknown soldier" (see Kathrin Asper's commentary), who died somewhere and nowhere, without anyone's company, and whose grave site remained unknown. When one of these grave sites is still found after decades, it is a moving experience for relatives, almost like taking someone home. I have witnessed this several times with people affected by such events. A picture like this can thus be a memorial site, a memorial sheet!

041 BOAF · "War: I. Death. 1939-1945"
Anonymous, undated, gouache on thin board, 24.7 x 17.4 cm
Picture Archive of the C.G. Jung Institute Zürich-Küsnacht

The Dead

The caption for this picture, too, reads "War:Death" (041 BOAH) and it was expressly composed as a commemorative painting, dedicated to all the unknown who were killed: "Commemorating those who were nameless, lost, buried in freezing loneliness! 1941-1945." It seems to have been painted after the war and focused on the time when the war against Russia was extended, which included the catastrophe in Stalingrad; freezing winters caused people to die from hunger and cold not only in Eastern Europe, but also in Germany. The painter commemorates those who died in eternal solitude, without companions, without a funeral in Russia's undiscoverable vastness. By commemorating them, they are lifted from oblivion – even within herself – into her deep and heartfelt memory: it is a reprocessing of grief in particular, and of trauma that this period of time and all the related losses of people have brought in their wake. We do not know for certain, but there were probably loved ones among the victims so that this picture may be an expression of a very personal form of grief.

Colors of ice and snow dominate the painting – white, gray-blue and gray-beige. It is pervaded by drifting snow, descending into the picture from the upper left – where fateful forces are often at work in a symbolic sense – and diagonally crossing the pictorial landscape from the gray sky that reaches down to the ground. In the bottom part of the picture, lifeless people, frozen to death, are lying on the snow, on a frozen lake. Five of them are visible. The body closest to the observer on the left is lying on the side, turned away from us, but his arms still seem to reach out in search for someone who might help him. To no avail. It is only in our memories, in commemoration that the painter and observers can be close to him.

041 BOAH · "War: III. Death. Commemorating those who were nameless, lost, buried in freezing loneliness! 1941–1945"
Anonymous, undated, gouache on thin board, 24.7 x 17.4 cm
Picture Archive of the C.G. Jung Institute Zürich-Küsnacht

Destroyed Building

In this picture of destruction (041 BOAX), painter and observer alike gaze down into the interior of a completely destroyed residential building. A structure is still towering on the right. It might indicate the original height of the building that could well have had multiple floors. Charred trees rear up on the side, now resembling bent steel rods. The destroyed building's interior is filled with crumbled boulders that came tumbling down during its destruction, right down to the place where people once lived and felt safe and secure. A black panel on the ground hints to the existence of a room, or is it the roof that has fallen down? A large ladder is lying on top of the ruins; it might have served as a neighborly access, a connection between the buildings. Parts of the structure are now scattered above and below. The building may have been hit by an explosive bomb which differs from a fire bomb in its explosive effect. A fire bomb has obviously hit the neighboring structure, unleashing a giant smoke cloud. Towards the front of the picture, right in the middle, we see remainders of the outside wall: huge sandstone-colored square stones. Glancing over them, we realize the depth of the bombing. The rooms in the basement might also have been destroyed, precisely where residents used to seek protection from the war bombing.

If we asked ourselves why the painter has devoted herself with such diligence to the depiction of the interior, it is again the symbolic space in the painting we need to look at. The picture's lower right quadrant is the very location where the aspect of safety and security usually appears. Here, personal safety and security have been targeted, perhaps the painter's own home, her own apartment at the time.

Dominating the view is a huge, black-gray plume of smoke, ascending at the left end of the destroyed structure, with the visible part of the street also leading in this direction. As already noted, a fire bomb must have hit this spot. The smoke fills the entire upper part of the painting, covering the fire-red sky and moving towards the upper right corner, thus occupying the entire upper right quadrant. In this way, it literally devours and suffocates the space where the symbolic future is located in this picture. On the left, we see a towering ruin, ossified, with charred beams. In the symbolic context of the painting, it is in the zone of the collective memory, the collective unconscious. It becomes obvious that here, too, it is only destruction that can be memorized and experienced in this area. Access to the deep and healing realms and symbols of the collective unconscious is still blocked for the painter at this point in time.

The creator has titled her picture "De profundis" – "From the depths", and added 1945 as the year, which also marks the end of the war. It is from the depths of the destroyed buildings that this painting has emerged. At the same time, the title alludes to the psalm verse: "...from the depths of my heart...."

041 BOAX · "De profundis!"
Anonymous, 1945, gouache on thin board, 24.7 x 17.4 cm
Picture Archive of the C.G. Jung Institute Zürich-Küsnacht

Fugitives

Two people have come very close to us in this painting (041 BOAI), facing us at the front of the picture. The right person, standing at the very edge of the composition, has already crossed this border, the bottom margin of the picture, moving towards the observer. The long hair reveals that she is a woman. It is from this perspective that she seems to have come even closer to us. The tall slim woman is not looking at us, but has unmistakably positioned herself right in front of the observer with her rucksack, probably carrying all her belongings. She could be one of the "bombed-out" people, how we used to call them back then, or they are both fugitives. Her left hand is placed in front of her breast, level with the heart, while the right one reaches out to her companion who has sunken to his knees beside her, covering his face with his hands. He does not want to be seen in this misery – or is he crying? Two heavy black spheres on his left are again redolent of the burden and the inner imprisonment of these people dressed in black. They have fled the town and crossed the endless plain, while the fiery glow continues to hover over the city on the horizon, morphing into black smoke clouds.

These are two of the millions of homeless, who, like so many of us at the time and like so many of us today, have seen their homes gone up in flames. They were hardly able to save their lives and now stand there, not knowing where to turn to. Although we do not know any details, the painter herself might have experienced this in a similar way. The firestorm in the picture is moving to the right, into the future. After 1945, the war might have ended in the outside world, but it certainly lingered on for a very long time inside the painter.

041 BOAI · "Homeless! 1939–1947"

Anonymous undated, gouache on thin board, 24.7 x 17.4 cm
Picture Archive of the C.G. Jung Institute Zürich-Küsnacht

Destroyed Metropolis

The picture's caption reads: "The Tombstone. After the Catastrophe. 1945. Impression of a Metropolis in Germany" (041 BOAL). It was composed by the painter in the face of the catastrophe at the end of the war in 1945 – under the imprint of a destroyed German metropolis – and illustrates that there were hundreds of thousands of fatalities in each of these cities. Like a heavy burden – in the landscape format – the horrific impression of a ruined city immersed in black becomes blatantly obvious: it is here, on both sides of the waters, a river, that we see jagged ruins; between them, as if hovering above the water, lies death, brightly gleaming in the guise of a white skeleton. Above the scene, a red sky, morphing and dying down into black. But covering the entire composition is a hovering black panel, probably envisioned as a single joint ledger as the picture's "tombstone." Death bridges a river. In each of the cities that were hit by the bombardments - and in my hometown as well -, a huge cemetery area had to be created, a large communal grave solely dedicated to those who died in these bombardments. Their numbers were countless, and they could not be identified because their bodies were torn and burnt.

041 BOAL · "The Tombstone. After the Catastrophe. 1945. Impression of a Metropolis in Germany"
Anonymous 1945, gouache on thin board, 24.7 x 17.4 cm
Picture Archive of the C.G. Jung Institute Zürich-Küsnacht

Extermination Camps

I have added the painting with the barbed wire here (041 BOAO), as it depicts the painter's concernment and even shock about the German guilt, the genocide at the time and the Holocaust against the Jews. She has titled her picture "Barbed Wire", referring to the years 1933-1947 as the period in question.

1933 was the very year Hitler seized power and already started installing concentration camps. Extermination camps for the so-called "final solution to the Jewish question", gas chambers and crematories were added in 1941. Unless it refers to a personal memory, the year 1947, however, could point to the year when on 30 September 1947 and 1 October 1947, the conviction of the chief perpetrators of the atrocities of the NS regime by an international military tribunal took place.

Parallel beams of barbed wire cross the composition and put the observer in a position directly in front of it. Behind the fence is the silhouette of a concentration camp: a prison-like concrete building, with a smoking chimney of an incinerator, expelling smoke into the fiery red sky. In the foreground, two persons killed while trying to escape are hanging in the high-voltage barbed wire of the concentration camp. The person on the right is entirely burnt, with his head hanging forward. On the left, a bare-chested young person is clasping the wire while still kneeling - a moving gesture. In the original painting, there is an oddly vivid play of light reflections on his torso, strongly contrasting the dominating somber gray shades of the rest of the picture. Are these reflections meant to express the longing for life that brought death to the young man upon touching the wire?

In a contemporary witness's report, Ruth Elias explains: "If someone approached the fence, he was shot at immediately. If he still managed to reach the fence, he instantly dropped dead because of the high voltage. Many preferred this kind of death to the horrifying life in the camps...."2 The painting is composed in a way that both the painter and the observer are directly and inevitably confronted with the barbed wire and the sight of the dead persons, who preferred to die in the fence rather than endure the humiliating and horrific life in the concentration camps. It unsparingly evokes feelings like shock, remembrance and deeply felt empathy. Could it be that the painter herself lost a loved one in this barbed wire or one of the camps? We do not know but cannot rule this out either. A feeling of deep shame about the fact that something like this could have happened at all among the human race, and what is more, in a country like Germany, hit me hard as a teenager. People my age, an entire generation born in this country, were repeatedly confronted with the unbelievable, not least through the information that was increasingly disseminated at schools.

041 BOAO · "Barbed Wire: 1933-1947!"
Anonymous, undated, gouache on thin board, 24.7 x 17.4 cm
Picture Archive of the C.G. Jung Institute Zürich-Küsnacht

Commemorating the Prisoners

This very dark and high room emanates a cold impression. The first thing we see is the tortured person tied to the pole, it being the most colorful and bright aspect in the painting, depicted from a perspective that seems to lift him high above the ground. He is still clinging on to the torturing pole (041 BOAN). Crouched by the left wall, a man seems to be waiting. Further to the right, sitting on the floor with her knees pulled tight, is obviously a woman, both fettered. Hans and Sophie Scholl instinctively come to mind, the more so because "Munich" is explicitly mentioned in the caption of the last picture of this series (041 BOAQ) – presumably the painter's home town and the location of the entire picture series. Together with other students and relatively early, around 1942/1943, the Scholl siblings had founded "The White Rose", a resistance group against the Hitler regime. In the background of this cold room, right in its center, a fourth tortured person becomes visible. Looking closer, we can identify him as Jesus Christ on the cross. Behind this sacrificing scene, which could also depict the imprisonment of the young students Hans and Sophie Scholl who were executed on 22 February 1943 in Munich-Stadelheim, is the cross, the symbol of Christ's co-suffering in this situation. Given the painter's Christian background, this was what she believed in, what she hoped for and relied on.

041 BOAN · "Commemorating the Imprisoned, Beaten and Fettered. 1933-1945"
Anonymous, undated, gouache on thin board, 24.7 x 17.4 cm
Picture Archive of the C.G. Jung Institute Zürich-Küsnacht

Commemorating the Tortured and Imprisoned

Another picture of commemoration, empathy and appreciation (041 BOAP), by which the traumatized painter also addresses and honors the tortured and captivated parts of herself, and in this way, might come a little closer to her grief and the healing of her psyche. This is an utterly dynamic painting of Christ: He is standing with his arms stretched out, as if reaching up into the sky, although his head is bowed. He is standing in front of a cross that only becomes visible on closer inspection of the background, painted in subtle purple and red-brown. Despite all the agony he must endure, the figure of Christ is very erect. Beams of energy are emanating from him, reaching the tortured person on the right with their full power. His face is immersed in this stream of light coming from the bent head of Christ and his tortured hands are likewise touched by the streams coming from Christ's hands. The anxious prisoner at the bottom of the picture, sitting on a low bench and covering his face with his hands, is reached by the beam of affection, streaming towards him from the wound on Christ's side, from the area around his heart.

The composition of this picture is very powerful and against its mainly dark background, a prison window also becomes visible upon closer inspection. The entire purple zone on the upper left, however, is accentuated like a large triangle above the remaining space of the picture and radiates an invincible force of life. In Germany, too, resistance rose – *deo concedente* – above the agony of countless victims of the NS regime that acted out of racist and ideological motives. As mentioned, the entire picture series is presumably related to the city of Munich, which should remind us once again of the students Hans and Sophie Scholl.

We see a gripping depiction that testifies to the heartfelt connection of the creative painter with the victims, but also with the symbol of Christ (as a symbol of redemptive co-suffering) that also becomes apparent in other paintings of hers which cannot be shown here in their entirety. It is a strong illustration of how this woman – amid the immense suffering around her – still experienced the connecting and consoling power of compassion. The two tortured persons find themselves in a state of profound desolation – and, yet again, they do not. They appear in the light, under the intense beaming and radiation emanating from the figure of Christ who has been crucified in this picture once again: from hands to hands, from face to face. Christ is sharing this prison cell with the tortured, but the cross he is hanging on seems to protrude into this cell from another dimension, so that his living energy is shared from wound to wound.

For people like us, the young generation, who had still witnessed the war and learned about and became aware of the real extent of the atrocities after the war had ended, the few witnesses of resistance were almost lifesaving. They gave hope to a renewed Germany, even to a renewed world. The date specifications on her pictures reveal that the painter was very aware, very afflicted and concerned by everything that people did to resist the Hitler regime, even if they had to sacrifice their own lives.

041 BOAP · "To the Tortured and Imprisoned 1933-1945!"
Anonymous,undated, gouache on thin board, 24.7 x 17.4 cm
Picture Archive of the C.G. Jung Institute Zürich-Küsnacht

Air Raid

A city – Munich? – in a rage of fire, 1943 (picture 126), when the air raids on German cities were mainly carried out by English and American bombers after the German Air Force had attacked cities like London in a similar way. I myself witnessed these events as a child. It started with the wailing of alarm sirens in this particular, high-pitched sound that became painfully sharp. The bombers were flying at a high altitude since the German flak defense was feared for being able to target and shoot down many of them. We could only hear their singing sound. And once you heard it, you had to drop everything, grab the bare necessities and what was important – for example, the youngest member of a family, the baby – in order to immediately rush into the nearest air-raid shelter, like a converted apple cellar. The first impacts usually occurred when we were still on the stairs and the ground started trembling. Electricity and water were cut immediately. We felt the ground shaking under the impacts and the air raid shelter filled with dust and smoke. After the all-clear signal, the house was burning or partially or completely destroyed. Everybody started to extinguish fires in their own or their neighbors' homes, even if they had been complete strangers up to this point, to free buried persons, to take care of injured and retrieve the dead. The fear of death we experienced during the air raids was solely alleviated by a huge wave of readiness to help, brought on by the imperative and the willingness to attend to those most in need.

In this picture, the horrors that exceeded common human capacity are depicted by someone who had without doubt experienced these events herself and superelevated them into the mystical. The fire is spit out by superhuman masks, blazing from their mouths, eyes and hair. The shocks of hair are painted as wafting firestorms, causing the city to burst into flames, as indicated by the structures lined in red. The fire is trickling into the buildings. The composition is divided into an upper and a lower half. The upper one shows the town's scenery, its church towers and skyscrapers, with some of them reminding of Munich. Brickwork is depicted in the bottom half that is separated by a fiery red line. The basement below the ground also seems to be visible here, whereto people fled from the attacks, but were still threatened, as the black dots and circles on the left indicate. These might be impacts, or traces of soot from the fires. On the right, the embers are bursting into the picture, impending to blast the protecting walls, and driving the people from the air raid shelters into the open so that they would not be suffocated.

It is in this depth, directly in front of the wall or almost embedded in it, that a mysterious figure appears. It has long blue hair that is falling down to its back and is covered in a light blue cape – the only blue item in the picture! The observer sees the back of this figure, standing there with its arms stretched out widely and the palms opened upwards, completely facing the wall and the city. This is in fact the oldest known praying gesture. Maria, the Virgin of Mercy, is oftentimes depicted in a blue vesture (also in a further painting of this series that we cannot show here due to lack of

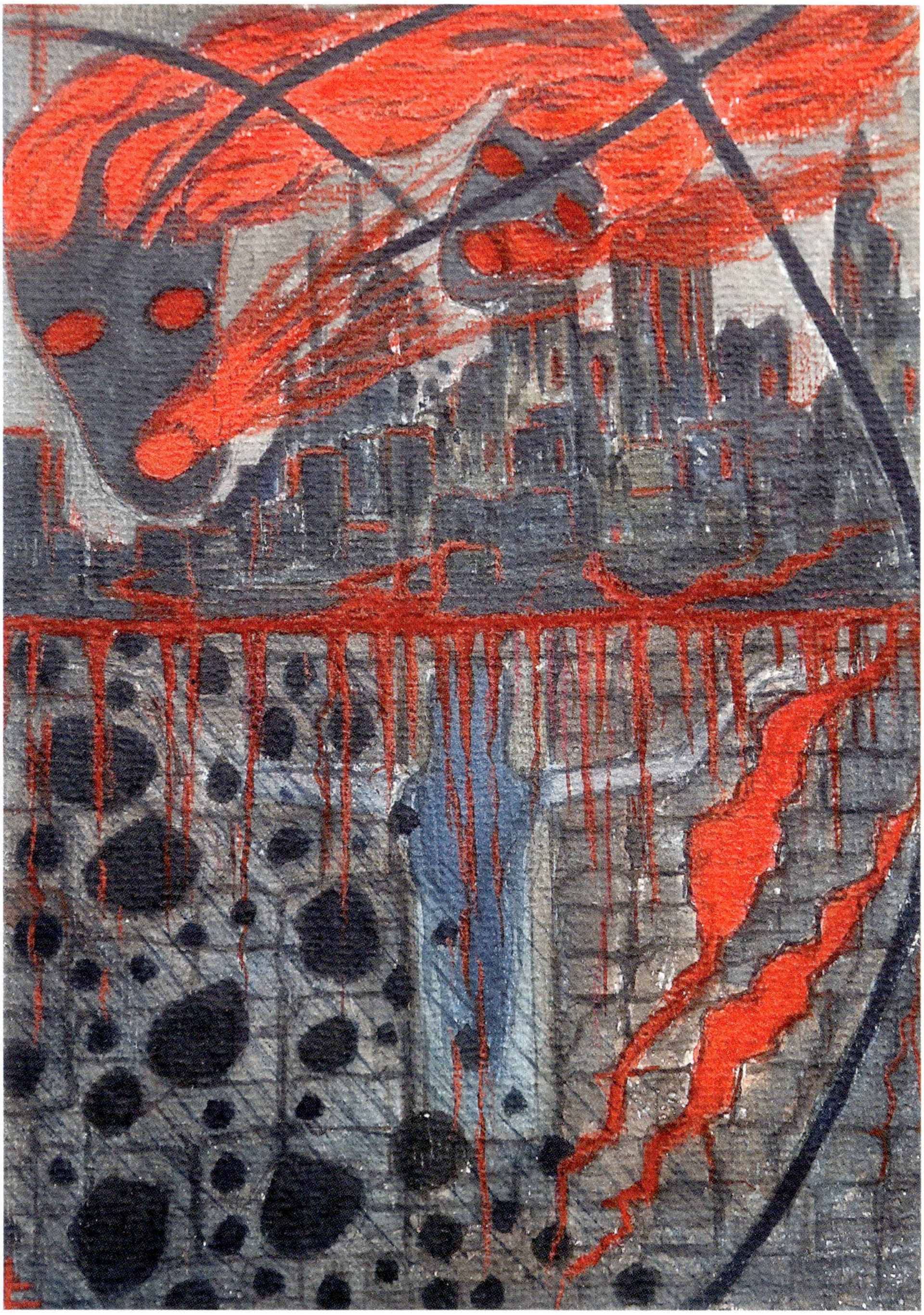

041 BOAR · "Alarm!! Fire Bombs and Attacks. The Air Raid during the War, 1943. Experiences"
Anonymous, , undated, gouache on thin board, 24.7 x 17.4 cm
Picture Archive of the C.G. Jung Institute Zürich-Küsnacht

space). It is also a gesture of prayer that is used in illustrations of the human soul when it is begging for protection. It is a depiction where in the face of the utmost and superhuman threat, a guardian is called upon that is larger than life: seen from this angle, it is also a picture of hope amid this boundless horror. It reminds me of the real, enormous, and devoted readiness to help among the affected people, which I was able to repeatedly witness as a child.

The Victim

The city of Munich, in which the painter presumably lived, is expressly mentioned here together with a specific date, namely 2 February 1945 (041 BOAQ). On this day, three further persons involved in the German resistance and the assault on Hitler on 20 July 1944 were sentenced to death: Klaus Bonhoeffer, Ernst von Harneck and Rüdiger Schleicher. The hanged person (on the crossbeam of a high T-cross, to the right of the central axis of the composition) is probably one of the partisans. Lonely, with his hair shining brightly and dressed in white, he is hanging near the center of the picture. His clothes are white, the color of pureness, probably underlining his innocence in this sacrifice. In the same way, the high cross at his side might stand for the innocence in the sacrifice made by Christ. Both are meant to bring salvation: "The Victim" is the title that the painter has chosen for her work. Her central motif is to see these executions as a sacrifice – for Germany's liberation? This needs to be considered in the context of a severely damaged sense of identity and self-esteem of young Germans like us in the post-war period.

Sophie Scholl is only one example of highly esteemed women and men who paid for their resistance with their lives - back then and nowadays more than ever! Despite all the horror depicted in this composition, it still emanates a certain calm. The wounded city is arranged in a shell-like manner around the cross. A circle-shaped colored patch beams above the scene in a fiery red like a – setting? – sun. The year is 1945! To my mind, this colored area is already breathing in the energy of the rising sun, also caused by the deeds of those who sacrificed their lives for a new beginning. This is mainly testified to by the dynamic composition of the painting, in which the power of the redly gleaming sun succeeds to continue into the blue-black sky. The bloodstreams at the foot of the cross permeate the solid darkened black soil, but appear to be living roots with blood flowing through them.

The sun is going to rise over the hanged person. He appears in the white clothing of the innocently hanged, of someone who has sacrificed himself. His shock of hair is the brightest glimmer of light in this composition. The hanged person is not fixed just somewhere, but to a towering T-cross. Yet it has a crossbar at the top and no extension of the central axis protruding into the sky. The symbolic meaning can be found in the experience itself: everything that happened during this time had to be endured in the material, mundane world, in the immanence of the humane. Theologist Dietrich Bonhoeffer himself was deeply affected by this experience, namely that in those apocalyptic times, the almighty protecting God could no longer be experienced in his transcendence.

041 BOAQ · "The Victim. Munich 1945! Impressions – Vision"
Anonymous, 2 February 1945, gouache on thin board, 24.7 x 17.4 cm.
Picture Archive of the C.G. Jung Institute Zürich-Küsnacht

He therefore suspected that the act of compassion was the only way to still find a transboundary and liberating experience.

The repeated act of compassion that also took place in painting these events and sharing them during the therapy sessions with Jung might entail the therapeutic effect in this mourning.

Notes

[1] C. G. Jung, *Memories, Dreams, Reflections*, 133-135.

[2] Ruth Elias, *Triumph of Hope*.

References

Elias, Ruth: *Triumph of Hope*, John Wiley & Sons, 1998, New York.

Jung, C. G., *Memories, Dreams, Reflections*. Recorded and edited by Aniela Jaffé. Special edition. Fontana Press, London, 1995, 200.

—— *Das Rote Buch. Der Text.* Herausgegeben und eingeleitet von Sonu Shamdasani. Vorwort von Ulrich Hoerni. Einleitung, Hinweise des Herausgebers zur Edition, Anmerkungsapparat und Danksagung aus dem Englischen von Christian Hermes. Philemon Series. Patmos, Ostfildern 2017, S. 133-135.

A New Configuration of the World

A DRAWING FROM THE PICTURE ARCHIVE

Philip Ursprung

TODAY THE BRIDGE BETWEEN the realm of art as an autonomous practice and artistic activity for therapeutic purposes is hardly traversed anymore. Art, science, medicine and psychology, like all realms of knowledge, have become increasingly specialized and delineated since the middle of the 20th century. This, however, was not always the case. In the second half of the 19th century the boundary zone between the disciplines of knowledge was one of the most vital places of thought. It was not the specialists who drew the most attention but those who tried to understand the world in its totality. Charles Darwin explored the beginnings and the development of all forms of life. Charles Lyell elucidated the emergence of mountains and continents. Henri Bergson overcame the philosophical distinction between idealism and realism. Sigmund Freud identified the laws of the human psyche. Marie Curie transcended the boundaries between physics and chemistry, and Albert Einstein linked the dimensions of time and space. To this day, these synthetic models of thought are both fascinating and inspiring. They offer an anti-type picture to today's segregated landscape of science. Of course even today there are still connections between art and psychology. Concepts from psychology such as 'the unconscious', 'archetypes', 'transference' are terms commonly used even in art. Some art theorists make use of the methodology of psychology, be it the terminology of Carl Gustav Jung or Freud or Jacques Lacan's studies, such as those issues related to the gaze. The influential documenta 5 exhibition in Kassel in 1972 included a section on the theme of "artistic production by psychiatric patients." The Collection de l'Art Brut in Lausanne, the Museum Gugging located on the grounds of the former Provincial Psychiatric Clinic in Gugging, the Prinzhorn Collection in Heidelberg, the Museum im Lagerhaus in St. Gallen, the Adolf-Wölfli Foundation at the Kunstmuseum Berne all contain collections of artworks by patients and also exhibit them. And the 58th Art Biennale in Venice in 2013 prominently displayed C.G. Jung's Red Book as part of the thematic exhibition titled "The Encyclopedic Palazzo." But, clearly, all of these cases were exceptions, focusing on "art brut", as the artist Jean Dubuffet called it, or "Outsider Art," which is strictly separated from art's actual canon.1

At present, architecture is better able than art to build bridges with other disciplines. The affinity

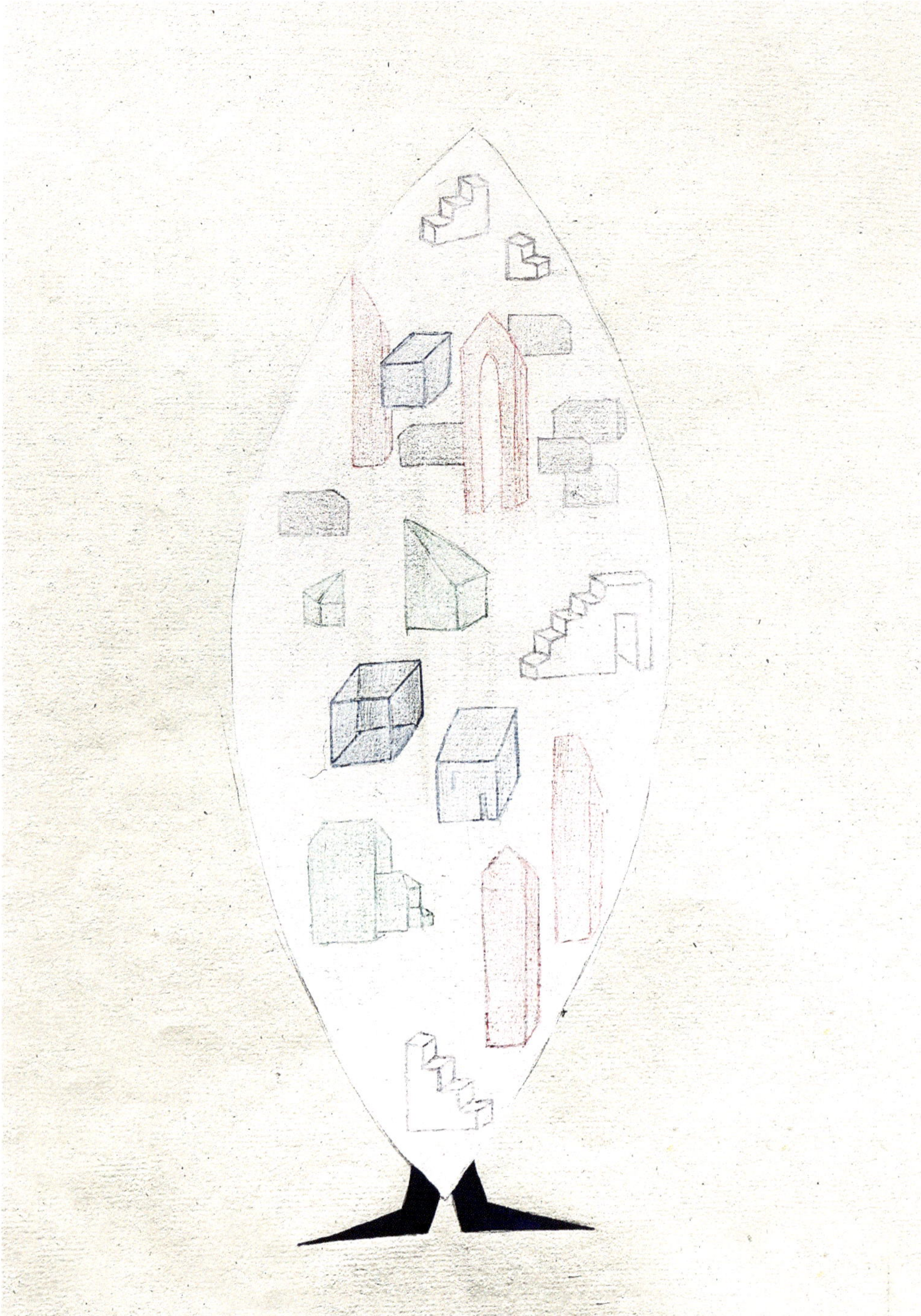

009 AIBH

between architecture and psychology is apparent, even though it is, surprisingly, hardly described. Among all the fields of knowledge architecture as well as psychology has been least susceptible to the trend of specialization. In the industrial nations both are among the most popular fields of study, that is, young people see them as promising areas in the future. The popularity of architecture and psychology also lies in the fact that both continue to be universal practices, in which various realms of knowledge converge. Architects deal with buildings – from the very first idea to planning, execution to the aging of materials. Psychologists have a personal connection with people over an extended period of time, following a process of learning and healing. It thus comes naturally for me as a historian of art and architecture to venture out onto the rather neglected bridge I mentioned at the outset and to explore what my discipline can learn from this encounter.

Art and Therapy

When Ruth Ammann, my godmother, suggested that I write about several documents stemming from the Picture Archive in connection with drawings by patients of C.G. Jung I first had to overcome some inner inhibitions. Our interests have overlapped for a long time. She, a trained architect, only discovered psychology later on. I am trained as an art historian specializing in architecture. Still, I was a bit reluctant since I wasn't sure that the categories and terms that are used in art could be so simply applied to psychology and psychiatry. An artwork must be exhibited in order to really exist, that is, has to be viewed by the public, and it cannot be compared with a sketch that no one but the patient and the doctor sees. The latter, produced by a patient, is an intimate expression, one that is only possible with the trust ensured by confidentiality and a protected setting. An artwork increases complexity, as the sociologist Niklas Luhmann has noted, whereas a therapeutic drawing is intended to reduce complexity. How can I compare something that the person who created it intended to be definitive and completed, for everyone to see now and in posterity, with something that emerged as a tool in a therapeutic conversation – intended to become obsolete once the problem is resolved?

If the patients' drawings are seen as part of visual culture, which includes not only the visual arts but also films, popular culture, and the visual representations of science, then they become more accessible. But I was still reluctant for another reason. Artists have long fought for the autonomy of their work – if you will, since the end of the *Ancien Régime* in the late 18th century when the earlier function of art as a commissioned artifact gave way to art for art's sake. This type of art was traditionally supposed to revise and further develop prevailing norms and the art that preceded it. Throughout history critics and detractors of the art of a given time have countered this view with the argument that they are abnormal, signs of a disturbance. The history of modern art stands under the sway of verdicts pathologizing artworks – from the scathing review of Edouard Manet's paintings in Paris of the 1860s, the propaganda exhibition

Degenerate Art in 1937 to the hostile reactions to Christoph Schlingensief's performances. Genius and madness are closely allied in the perception of the vast majority. To this day the first thing most people associate with Vincent van Gogh is the fact that he cut off one ear. As an art historian I almost instinctively protest when someone interprets an artwork as a "symptom."

When Ruth Ammann showed me some of the drawings my curiosity was piqued. Engaging with something new, unfamiliar always broadens one's horizon. I couldn't say why but when I saw the pictures I found it less restricting and more liberating to view the drawings with the eyes and instruments of an art historian. A drawing, dated 1929, immediately grabbed my attention. (009 AIBH)The sheet shows a whitish figure rendered in a very schematic manner, as a lenticular form standing on two stylized black feet. On the inside of this lenticular figure one sees twenty geometric bodies that are schematically depicted, drawn with red, violet, and blue colored pencils. There are clear outlines. This and the fact the drawing is dated – even if I'm not sure whether it's by the person who drew it or by C.G. Jung, the doctor and therapist – indicates that it can be seen as completed. From the order of the files we also know that it is a single sheet, that it is not part of the series that had been drawn ten years earlier.

As an art historian I work with analogies, which means that I compare something unknown with something I already know. One of the premises of art historiography is that forms, shapes have a separate life and can appear at various places in the course of history. The book by the art historian Henri Focillon, *The Life of Forms* (1934), the book by his student Georg Kubler, *The Shape of Time* (1962) and projects such as Aby Warburg's collection of documents as part of the "Mnemosyne atlas" project are attempts to systematize this intrinsic dynamic.[2] The lenticular figure – it emerges from the intersection of two circles – could allude to a body or a head or even a vertical eye. It could also be associated with the form of the vagina, a window or mirror, or even a spear, a projectile. Such lenticular representations of bodies, heads or eyes recur again and again in the art of the 1920s, as for instance in the oeuvres of Paul Klee, Constantin Brancusi, Sophie Taueber-Arp, or Alberto Giacometti.

Mandorla

The motif of the lenticular or almond form was also widespread in late antiquity and in the Middle Ages. As a "Mandorla" it surrounds the body of Christ. The motif can be found on altars, in manuscripts, on frescoes, ivory carvings and reliefs, most prominently in the tympanum of the main portal of the cathedral in Chartres. (Fig. 1). It underscores Christ hierarchically, delineating him from the other saints. The motif, however, can also be read as a sign of a vision, of an apparition. The best-known artwork in the German-speaking world in the time around and following World War I was Matthias Grünewald's *Isenheim Altar*. The most frequently reproduced motif of the altar was the panel depicting the resurrection of Christ who, surrounded by an aureola, recalling the mandorla,

Fig. 1. Christ contained within a mandorla, ca. 1150
(Middle portal, west facade, Chartres Cathedral)

Fig. 2. Matthias Grünewald, Isenheim Altar, 1506-1515
(Colmar, Unterlinden Museum)

rises up against the dark background. (Fig. 2) In its time, the painting was just as much a part of collective memory as Andy Warhol's *Marilyn* is today.

The geometric bodies drawn within the lenticular figure (009 AIBH) allude to architectural elements, staircases, house sections, doors, gates. They are rendered as free-floating, without any mooring. There is no allusion to a ground. The arrangement and the motifs are redolent of some of Paul Klee's paintings and drawings, which also depict stylized architectural elements such as towers, gates, roofs, paths, staircases, windows.

The geometrical bodies also resemble elements from a architectural building box, like the Anker Stone building blocks developed by pedagogue Friedrich Fröbel. These popular building boxes, consisting of small cast stones in the primary colors, could be found in every child's room between the late 19th and middle 20th century. They could be used to erect small buildings, without the use of glue, based entirely on statics, and then knocked down again.

As an art historian I am also reminded of even earlier works such as the architectural fantasies of Giovanni Battista Piranesi at the end of the 18th century. In his famous etchings, Piranesi captured *vedutas* of cities, most notably in Rome. He was particularly fascinated by the ancient ruins, the colossal relics of past glory. His fantastic architectural renditions, such as the *Carceri*, imaginary prison landscapes, (Fig. 3) depict mysterious architectures, corridors that disappear into a void, steps that lead to podiums, vaults towering one on top of the other. These are incredibly complex spaces where inside and outside are often not clearly separated. The viewer is confronted with images believed to be familiar from dreams, connections between ruins and construction sites, order and chaos.

I cannot say – and it is also irrelevant to the matter at hand – whether the person who created the drawing had a mandorla in mind, whether he or she was familiar with the work of Piranesi, Klee, or others. The assuredness of depiction, the clarity of composition, the sovereign arrangement of the figure in relation to the edge of the sheet – and the comparison with the earlier series from Jung's files – make it seem highly plausible that this person had received artistic training and was not simply dabbling in art.

How can I now interpret the drawing? What can my discipline learn from it – and by the same token what can I teach psychology? There is no title, that is, I cannot go by what the drawer intended nor does Jung's interpretation help us. If we take the mandorla as the framework for a vision, then we can plausibly see the figure, which stands on firm feet, if not on firm ground – as the image of a vision, a dream.

Are the architectural elements signs of destruction, or elements of reconstruction? If we look closely, all elements appear neatly rendered, all intact. There is nothing indicating destruction. I thus do not interpret them as part of an entire structure in ruins but as building blocks for a construction, albeit one that is still unfinished and not defined. It is a discontinuous space, one that contains the possibility of coherence, but with an outcome that is still uncertain.

Fig. 3. Giovanni Battista Piranesi, "Carceri III" (The Round Tower), *Imaginary Prisons*, 1761

Crash

Since the drawing is untitled, I will focus – this, too, being an art historian's automatic reaction – on the date. The year 1929 is a date that has inscribed itself in history. "Black Thursday" of October 24, 1929 stands for the greatest catastrophe in the history of capitalism – the crash on the New York Stock Exchange. The crash had long been in the making but in the final days of October, when investors scrambled to withdraw their bonds, the stock market crashed.

This marked the beginning of the Great Depression in the U.S. and triggered a worldwide economic crisis. As an art historian I am interested in how an instance of economic-historical turmoil, that is, a change in the understanding and representation of value, is reflected in the images of the time. I do not mean to say that art "expresses" or "illustrates" historical changes. Rather, I would argue that the visual arts anticipate such changes long before they can be conceptually grasped.

A therapeutic drawing that taps into the unconscious is particularly well suited to serve as a source for capturing not just the individual dimension but also a more general one.

From my perspective as a historian of art and architecture I am interested in the drawing as a kind of lens that offers me a clearer view of the changes taking place at a certain time. So I do not interpret it just as a glance into the inner world of a person but – as already alluded to above – as a framework and a reflection of a trend that transcends the individual. Seen from this perspective, the lenticular figure could be interpreted as a vision of a world that has lost its moorings, has come apart. The existing structure has dissolved, the edifice of the world economy has collapsed, falling into many pieces. The elements drift freely, with no connection within an unstructured space. The representational system has been turned upside down, just as if gravity had been temporarily abolished and all elements were floating in space. Yet the elements are still clearly recognizable as such. It is entirely conceivable that they could be reconfigured. The world that has dissolved into many pieces could also be reconstructed again from all of these pieces.

The vision of the eye shape drawn by Jung's patient differs in this sense from the scene in *The Andalusian Dog*, the film made by Luis Bunuel and Salvador Dalì that same year (1929). It is a famous scene, perhaps just as known today as the vision depicted on the Isenheim Altar was in its time. It is a large close-up of a woman's eyeball being slit with a razor blade. No one who has seen this scene will ever forget it. Not just because it is something one doesn't dare to imagine but also because an old representational system is being radically expunged here.

If I connect this particular scene with the crash that took place just a few months later, then I can interpret it as showing that the prevailing representational system has been rendered irreversibly obsolete. By contrast, the process that was reflected in the vision depicted by the patient's drawing, is unclear, but in essence reversible, in the sense that the status quo can be restored again.

Active Imagination

Both in Bunuel's and Salvador Dali's Surrealist film and in the drawing of the lenticular figure, my association with the economic catastrophe is hypothetical. I cannot prove it. But I can argue that what these images show is something that cannot be conceptually grasped.

C.G. Jung's method of active imagination is of great interest in this connection. According to Jung, the method is only successful if the patients allow an inner image that has taken shape over a long period, like a dream image, to transform before it is described in words.

If the inner images are conceptually grasped too soon, then the unconscious does not have a chance to analyze the patient.[3] The inner image has to remain intact, untouched by linguistic representation, until it changes, by itself as it were, and has an effect on the individual. A similar process takes place when I interpret an artwork. Here the work is not an inner image or a dream image but an artwork that was created by someone with a specific intention and idea and it is something that exists in a physical, tangible sense. But also with an artwork, one does not get around viewing it, engaging with it in a more intensive way.

With an artwork, the perceived and imagined images dissolve and here, too, the meaning should not be too quickly set down. Each definition – for instance the categorization in terms of a stylistic concept, the attribution to an author, the reduction to the depicted material – limits the scope of possible meanings. An interpretation should not just offer ample room for the reader's fantasy, it should also leave the leeway to the viewer and stimulate their fantasy. In the best case, the meaning is forthcoming, moving constantly back and forth between the interpreter, object, and reader or viewer.

The architectural design process shows even greater affinity to Jung's method of active imagination than the process of interpretation. In the design stage, that is, the central phase of defining a form, there is a constant back and forth between image and concept, sketch, and language. In almost all architectural schools and firms, the design is based on so-called concept models, i.e., small three-dimensional, highly abstract models made of cardboard or foam that make it possible to literally pass on ideas from one hand to the next, and to test, reject or further develop them. Working with such models combines the visual with the tactile, since spatiality is always experienced with one's fingers and hands.

While in therapy the movement proceeds from patient to the image and back, then from patient to therapist and back, in architectural design it goes from architect to object and continues on to another architect. It is, unlike the visual arts, a collaborative process, a cooperation of at least two designers. This might explain why my inner inhibitions to deal with the subject of the therapeutic drawing, disappeared as soon as I actually saw the drawings. The process finally seemed familiar to me, since I knew it in another guise from the architectural design process.

It is rewarding for both experts and amateurs to observe someone drawing or painting. Just as people stop and look when a building is constructed or a street artist portrays passersby, it is hardly possible to escape the fascination of drawing in the making. The same is true for design and – with some historical distance – for viewing series of pictures stemming from therapeutic processes. What makes this rewarding is the fact we can witness the play between the pre-conceptual and the conceptual, the unconscious and the conscious, the possible and the real. In this process meaning is being created, transformed and left open. The option ultimately selected is only one of many. The process is interrupted by the completion of therapy or the deadline for an architectural design but basically it could continue endlessly. Design just like analysis can, in essence, never end. That is what makes for its beauty and vitality.

Notes

[1] Cf. Angela Fink, *Kunst in der Psychiatrie: verklärt, verfolgt, vermarktet.* Vienna/Berlin/Münster: Lit Verlag, 2012.

[2] Henri Focillon, *The Life of Forms in Art.* Cambridge: MIT Press, 1992.;George Kubler, *The Shape of Time: Remarks on the History of Things.* New Haven, CT: Yale University Press, 1962; Aby Warburg, *Der Bilderatlas Mnemosyn.*, Berlin: Akademie Verlag, 2000.

[3] Cf. Jung's statements regarding active imagination in a letter (Three Letters to Mr. O., *Letters* vol. 1 (1947): May 2, 1947: "Thus you can not only analyse your unconscious but you also give your unconscious a chance to analyse yourself, and therewith you gradually create the unity of conscious and unconscious without which there is no individuation at all.")

In Closing

PAINTING FROM THE UNCONSCIOUS TODAY

Ingrid Riedel

The Picture Archive of the C.G. Jung Institute Zürich

In his day, C.G. Jung was the only well-known psychologist who intentionally painted pictures himself and created sculptures in the context of his own inner development. *The Red Book,*[1] which has been available to the public since 2008, is an impressive testimony of his artwork and his related thoughts and associations. He also motivated and encouraged many of his patients as early as 1917 to create pictures around their dreams and fantasies in order to facilitate access to their unconscious and explore the symbolic matter derived from it.

The Picture Archive of the C.G. Jung Institute Zürich in Küsnacht was established during Jung's last years of life before he passed away in 1961. Jolande Jacobi is probably the analyst of the Institute who was most interested in the possibilities that therapeutic artwork offered. She put together the collection that comprised more than 10,000 pieces (also see article by Vicente L. de Moura in this book). The earliest of the dated works of the Archive were created in 1917, the others in the roughly 40 years that followed. It was important to Jung that patients kept their artwork for repeated contemplation and did not pass it on, so that some of the paintings from his collection could well be copies, produced by their original creators. The pieces from Jacobi's therapeutic practice, however, are all original paintings. She saw copies in a more critical light, as the initial emotional impulse for painting was missing in this kind of work; hence, she certainly had her own concepts and ideas with a view to the Archive.

It was Jolande Jacobi who started to systematically categorize the entirety of the artwork according to generic terms and topics, while trying to identify the archetypal symbols behind the shapes and figures. This endeavor is ongoing to date, particularly with regard to the pictures from her own practice, even though curators from the Archive – volunteers from the Institute's current teaching staff - have increasingly dedicated their time to this undertaking.

The intention behind the extensive picture collection has been and still is to provide inspirational material from the origins of Painting Therapy to students, teachers and scholars in the field, and to find access to the language of the unconscious while contemplating the paintings. The cases which have to this day remained without any detailed context as to their creators (gender, age and reason for therapy) – like many from the Jacobi Collection – can only be interpreted to a certain extent. Nevertheless, they still convey the symbolism and archetypal concepts of the unconscious that are being expressed in psychotherapeutic processes. They also convey an authentic notion of what Jung himself saw or did get to see in his practice. The contributions in this book are vivid illustrations thereof. Some events, for example the bomb war from 1941-1945 (see my article), might have affected Jung on a deep emotional level.

The Origins of Painting Therapy According to C.G. Jung and Jolande Jacobi

Apart from her engagement in the establishment and utilization of the Picture Archive, Jolande Jacobi was the very person to summarize Jung's idea of the therapeutic effectiveness of painting and creative work in an initial concept of Jungian Painting Therapy. After a few attempts in the form of essays, she introduced the concept in her book *Vom Bilderreich der Seele* [*The Pictorial Realm of the Soul*][2] in 1969, in which she also elaborated on the extensive number of possible applications in psychotherapeutic practice. In this book, she categorizes 196 paintings from her own collection with a view to the respective painters and their comments on their work. She further describes their clinical picture and autobiographical topics by relating the latter to the painting's presentation and symbolism. In this manner, she offers a vivid insight into therapeutic processes around working with pictures. To date, Jacobi's classical text book is still not outdated, because it also serves as a workbook for Painting Therapy on the basis of Jungian psychotherapy, and contains all the components necessary to understand "pictures from the unconscious" – an expression coined by Jung – and their careful interpretation.

Jolande Jacobi, née Skekaks, was born in Hungary and completed her psychological studies – one of Jung's requirements for working at his institute – with a PhD degree in Vienna around 1934. Her mentors were Charlotte and Karl Bühler, and she had been in contact and trained with C.G. Jung since 1927. As a psychologist, she already knew about the findings of psychiatric-psychological research into the pictorial expression of mental problems at the time, although the focus was mainly on diagnostic work and research. Back then, the pioneering standard works on drawings and paintings of "the mentally ill" by Hans Prinzhorn, Walter Morgenthaler and Hans Oskar Pfister[3] were already accessible. Test psychology had already been developed and graphology[4] with its spatial symbolism and schemata was a highly esteemed method. Jacobi tried to apply graphological schemata to the spatial symbolism of paintings and drawings. As one of Jung's most prominent students, she was particularly qualified to recognize and establish the revolutionary concept of Painting Therapy on the basis of Jungian Analytical Psychology, as this new tool was all about integrating the unconscious into the painting process, and interpreting the connection between the unconscious and the conscious mind.

Very early on, Jung had tried to also discern the

patients' psychological state of mind from their pictorial works. His encounter with Indologist Heinrich Zimmer[5] in 1926 was a vital impulse for his understanding of "pictures of the soul" from a psychoanalytical point of view. Zimmer held that in order to have an effect, such a picture needed "a shape (geometric Yantra), a gestalt, a meaningful message, and not least the genuine disposition with which it can be created and observed (translation from the original)."[6] As early as 1929, Jung described his method of encouraging creative painting in therapeutic practice in his essay "Aims of Psychotherapy"[7]. In another essay – "A Study in the Process of Individuation"[8] – written several years later, he likewise stated that he would encourage his patients to "paint in reality what they have seen in dreams or fantasies."[9] This was not supposed to be about art, but about something More and Different, about a "living effect upon the patient himself."[10] The very process of creation was seen by Jung as a way of Active Imagination: "Moreover, the concrete shaping of the Picture enforces a continuous study of it in all its parts , so that its effect can be developed to the full."[11]

Painting Therapy contains an element that is close to consciousness, namely creative action, which is particularly apt for passing on visual imaginations to the conscious mind that have surfaced from the unconscious. The discussion and psychoanalytical interpretation of the picture between the creative patient and the psychotherapist will even deepen this process. In "Aims of Psychotherapy," Jung explains that "by painting himself, he gives shape to himself."[12] Seen from this perspective, each painting is a self-Picture, and working on the painting is tantamount to working on one's own inner nature. "The patient can make himself creatively independent through this method," even after finishing the supporting therapy: "For instance, a patient needs only to have seen once or twice how much he is freed from a wretched state of mind by working at a symbolical picture and he will always turn to this means of release whenever things go badly for him. In this way, something of inestimable importance is won – the beginning of independence, a step towards psychological maturity."[13]

Hence, Jung developed Zimmer's approach towards a detailed processing of the "pictures of the soul" even further in practice. In his last psychiatry lecture on "Schizophrenia"[14] in 1957, he reiterated the importance of creative expression for successful psychotherapeutic healing. Despite all the groundbreaking impulses he has given, however, Jung himself never did produce a summary of all these therapeutic aspects, nor did he develop a concept for Painting Therapy from a psychological and methodological point of view.

It was Jolande Jacobi who accomplished all of that. In the theoretical part of her foundational work *Vom Bilderreich der Seele* [*On the Pictorial Realm of the Soul*), she extensively discusses the aspects that may serve as guidelines for interpreting artwork. Picture series are used, *inter alia*, to illustrate the subsequent practical examples in the book that span a vast field of applications from a diagnostic point of view, e.g. for certain clinical conditions like compulsive behavior. Jacobi also discusses the treatment of severe identity crises, sometimes reaching far into the spiritual realm. One particular picture, created during the treatment of a negative mother complex in an 18-year-old girl and titled "The devouring mother,"[15] exemplifies the approach that Jacobi uses and recommends for the interpretation of every painting:[16] As a first step, the general impression and expression of the picture needs to be perceived, followed by the significance of the painting materials and techniques used, which she always defines in detail. The relationship between picture and space is then assessed from the perspective of spatial symbolism, similar to how graphology saw the spatial use of handwriting at the time. Of further significance are proportions, the organization of the picture, movements and directions of movement, as well as perspective. In addition, Jacobi always examines color quality, the ratio of the number between individual picture elements and, finally, the central features themselves and their individual and collective symbolism.

In her last chapter "Painting Therapy," Jolande Jacobi even develops an approach for group therapy, based on her experiences with groups of hospitalized patients. The chapter's introduction[17] contains a remarkable summary of what she considers the main aspects in her work with pictures:

> For more than 20 years, I have dedicated my work to establishing a systematic methodological interpretation of what Jung called 'pictures of the unconscious', with a particular view to diagnosing the state that the painter was in at the time of creation. I was able to gain valuable insights into their expressive and symbolic significance and into the background of my analysands' mental processes, thereby establishing invisible, new relationships with them. I was surprised to find that more often than not, transferences were triggered by the understanding of such pictures that led to a nonverbal, but all the more dynamic secret consensus within the unconscious realms of analysand and analyst. In this process, the Picture emerging from the analysand's unconscious touched the same or similar Picture still dormant in the analyst's unconscious, asking for a response, and in this way, causing an emotional harmony that triggered a sense of being understood (translation from the original).[18]

A deeper form of transference and countertransference is thus made possible by means of creation and joint observation of artwork in therapy.

It is not sufficiently known that Jolande Jacobi already experimented with group therapy based on Jung's model – which was in fact conceptualized as individual therapy –, in which each of the participants was able to bring their unconscious and their paintings into the supporting circle of the group.

The head of the Zürichberg Clinic at the time, Dr. Heinrich Karl Fierz, was open-minded enough to let her carry out experiments with groups of patients that varied in number (eight to fifteen) and in symptomatology.

In the final chapter of her book, Jolande Jacobi also describes her methods:[19] During the painting process, she already perceived the agreeable atmosphere surfacing from joint creation, and noticed that the topic also served as a catalyst, able to free individuals from their isolation.[20]

Jacobi goes on to describe her methods and strategies: "After a good hour, the pictures were shown around, discussed among the participants and commented on by myself in a brief or more elaborate way (translation from the original)."[21] She further explains that "apart from subtle remarks on the colors' symbolism, numbers, space, proportions, picture elements etc., I tried to carefully hint to the situational diagnosis to the extent that the picture allowed me to (translation from the original).[22]

Most of the times, the atmosphere was surprisingly cheerful, even if sometimes one of the participants took part in the process only very reluctantly and after being encouraged by the other group members, but to finally come to the conclusion: "Now that was interesting, I had imagined this to be entirely different! (translation from the original)"[23]

For the doubtlessly rather challenging topic of the 'devil', even though it has an archetypal background, a 40-year-old neurotic woman came up with a starfish-like creation.[24] This devil must have emerged from the depths. Jacobi notes: "The tentacle-shaped points of the leaves have something lambent, devilish to them, something tempting and dangerous that could indeed catch you (translation from the original)."[25] It is a devil that appears in the shape of a black-red blossom, or precisely as a starfish.

Another - 28-year-old - woman painted a fiery, lively devil: "This devil with its hooknose, the funny headdress, and the tailcoat tips is a dynamic figure marching through the fire (translation from the original)"[26] – a figure that resides in the unconscious of the painter herself, with the direction towards the left, more often than not, indicating that it is all about the inner life of the person, about the co-creator herself. This figure illustrates a new opportunity for the painter who had formerly suffered from severe anorexia, but was now on her way to healing.

Jolande Jacobi's picture "The devilish girl," as she called it, is proof of her distinct humor when she partakes and exposes herself in this joint act of creation, this initial form of group therapy. She remarks: "Quite obviously, I'm not a painting artist either. In the picture, the 'devilish girl' covers her eyes; but woe if she opens them! (translation from the original)"[27] This remark might have been taken up by the group members - whose newly created paintings she would have seen by opening her eyes - with a wink, and they might have perceived it in the same way.

Whether or not the group leader's participation in the group's painting process is beneficial or could prove irritating is something that would have to be discussed in the context of today's experiences with Jungian Painting Therapy. In a similar fashion, motifs such as the 'devil' or the 'witch', even though of archetypal origin, might not always be suited for a group. Jacobi's first attempt of a Jungian Group Painting Therapy is still impressive as a rough concept, and has remained groundbreaking to this day with a view to its fundamental elements – symbolic motifs and joint discussion of the paintings among the group members, but also with the group leader. Numerous paintings from these early group therapies are certainly part of the Picture Archive's treasures, albeit not always labeled as such. They are awaiting further exploration.

Further Development of Jungian Painting Therapy

In which way has the notion and concept of Jungian Painting Therapy developed since Jolande Jacobi's groundbreaking work? It indeed took some time, from 1969 to 1992, until Christa Henzler and I wrote about the concept of Analytical Painting Therapy in our book *Maltherapie. Eine Einführung auf der Basis der Analytischen Psychologie von C.G. Jung* [*Painting Therapy. An Introduction on the Basis of C.G. Jung's Analytical Psychology*]. Several editions of this methodological textbook have been published so far; an extended edition published in 2016 introduces for the first time a model for supervision of Painting Therapy on the basis of patients' artwork.[28] The book illustrates the exploration and integration of the unconscious in creative processes, and exemplifies how the connection between the conscious and the unconscious is brought about by means of discussing and interpreting pictures in the context of Analytical Therapy. The factors we consider effective in Painting Therapy are listed in the book as follows: (1) The creative process as such; (2) the process of imagination and symbolization that develops alongside the first process; (3) the process of discussion and interpretation; and (4) the process of encounter and transference that takes place during the third step. The major building blocks for the interpretation of pictorial works from the unconscious have been my previous studies on "Colors," "Shapes," and "Pictures."[29]

A profound and thoroughly reflected concept for Group Painting Therapy was introduced by Christa Henzler and myself in 2008 in our rather practical book *Malen in der Gruppe* [*Painting in the Group*],[30] after more than twelve years of experience with patients and groups in professional training. This work draws on approaches that we had already incorporated in our fundamental book *Maltherapie* [*Painting Therapy*].

Brigitte Dorst[31], another contributor, introduced concepts for group therapy based on Jungian psychology which she repeatedly described in a pioneering way by incorporating imagination, symbolism, and pictures in group therapy. Her latest book is called *Therapeutisches Arbeiten mit Symbolen. Wege in die innere Bilderwelt* [*Therapeutic Work with Symbols. Paths to the Inner Pictorial Realm*], 2nd updated and extended edition 2015.

It should be noted, though, that Susan Bach[32] had already started research on "spontaneous painting and drawing in the field of surgery" at clinics in London back in 1961, and later used her approach for children and groups of children suffering from leukemia. She also gained experience in the vast field of psychosomatics (this current project, the *Book of Pictures*, was also funded by the Susan Bach Foundation on her behalf).

C.G. Jung institutes in the German-speaking countries – particularly in Zürich and Stuttgart – have anchored and supported Painting Therapy based on Jung's and Jacobi's concepts, both in their training programs for future analysts and in research programs.

Rudolf Michel[33] elaborated a more detailed scheme for spatial symbolism in the framework of his seminars and lectures at the C.G. Jung Institute in Zürich, which profoundly contributed to the interpretation of pictures from the unconscious. He also substantiated this approach by means of numerous examples. We now know that the right bottom quadrant often shows a particular symbolism that reflects a sense of security - or insecurity, as the case may be.

Helen Ingeborg Bachmann explored the developmental phases of separation and individuation processes in early childhood on the basis of pictorial representations, and published the results in her work *Malen als Lebensspur* [*Painting as a Life Trail*][34] in 1985.

Ursula Baumgardt's illustrative book *Kinderzeichnungen – Spiegel der Seele* [*Children's Paintings – Mirror of the Soul*] [35] was published in the same year.

Starting with Ursula Eschenbach[36] in 1978, the C.G. Jung Institute Stuttgart has repeatedly paid particular attention to pictures in the developmental processes of children and adolescents. Renate Daniel's comprehensive book *Archetypische Signaturen im unbewussten Malprozess* [*Archetypal Signatures in the Process of Unconscious Painting*][37], published in 1993, can be cited as yet another example.

Further research carried out at the C.G. Jung Institute Zürich focused on the possibilities of Jungian Painting Therapy in the psychiatric field, such as Paul Brutsche's[38] study "Zur Bedeutung der Perspektive in Analysanden-Zeichnungen" [On the Significance of Perspective in Analysands' Pictures], published in 1979. It showed that remarkable conclusions can be drawn from the way perspective is used in the structure of the ego complex, e.g. in the case of psychoses.

Essentially new perspectives on the application of Painting Therapy in the field of psychoses are outlined in the diploma theses of Manfred Krapp[39] and Margitta Giera-Krapp[40]. In his paper "Die Gestaltungstherapie als Beitrag zur Psychotherapie bei Psychosen" ["Creative Therapy as a Contribution to Psychotherapy in the Case of Psychoses"], the former warns against the application of Painting Therapy in the case of acute psychoses, drawing on the groundbreaking work of Gaetano Benedetti.[41] In her work "Beitrag zur Therapie der frühen Störungen" ["Contribution to the Therapy of Early Disorders"], Margitta Giera-Krapp underlines the effectiveness of Painting Therapy, particularly during restitution phases of the ego following psychotic relapses in bipolar disorders. Manfred Krapp[42] also presented an impressive new study on painting with groups of psychiatric patients.

Creative therapy – a term coined by Günter Clauser[43] in 1960 – is nowadays incorporated to a greater extent into the concepts for in-patient psychotherapy, and mainly applied in areas and methods of treatment of psychosomatic disorders. With regard to out-patient therapy, Painting Therapy has proven particularly successful in the treatment and post-treatment of addictions, anxiety disorders, in depressive persons, and not least in persons with narcissistic disorders.

The discussion whether or not persons with narcissistic disorders – and the broad range of psychosomatic patients – are able to form symbols and thus, create pictures has been concluded thanks to the positive experiences with numerous patients from this clinical field in favor of the assumption that a basic ability for symbolization exists that, however, has to be encouraged by the therapist. It was Gertraud Schottenloher[44] who since publishing her doctoral thesis Das therapeutische Potential spontanen bildnerischen Gestaltens unter besonderer Berücksichtigung körpertherapeutischer Methoden [*The Therapeutic Potential of Spontaneous Creative Painting under Special Consideration of Body-therapeutic Methods*] has been able to prove and substantiate the effectiveness of Painting Therapy in patients with early-onset disorders in her works. For Schottenloher, the constellation of a so-called "mother field" or the positive mother complex, is the supporting structure for Painting Therapy, especially for groups.

Holgrid Gabriel's[45] study "Die Behandlung früher Störungen mit kunsttherapeutischen Mitteln aus der Sicht von C.G. Jung" [The Treatment of Early Disorders by Means of Art Therapy from a C.G. Jungian Point of View] is heading in a similar direction.

In his guideline "Introduction to Picture Interpretation According to C.G. Jung," published in 2005, Theodor Abt[46] presented a special method that has gained some attention, namely an ever more detailed picture interpretation from a psychoanalytical viewpoint.

Christa Henzler's[47] diploma thesis, published in 1985, also focused on "Aspekte der Maltherapie unter besonderer Berücksichtigung des tiefenpsychologischen Interpretations-Ansatzes" ["Aspects of Painting Therapy under Particular Consideration of the Interpretation Approach from a Psychoanalytical Point of View"]. Some of her results have been included in our book *Maltherapie* [*Painting Therapy*].

As of 2003, Linda Briendl's[48] studies have served as valuable contributions to Jungian Painting Therapy. Among other themes, she particularly explores the field of emotions and "Creativity as an Expression of Emotion."

Together with Christa Henzler, I published the book *Malen um zu überleben. Ein kreativer Weg durch die Trauer* [*Painting to Survive. A Creative Path through Mourning*][49] in 2004. The book was preceded by Henzler's essay on "Malen gegen den Tod. Die Funktion des Malens bei der Durchschreitung der Trauerphasen" ["Painting against Death. The Function of Painting in Moving through the Phases of Mourning"],[50] published in 2003.

When Flora von Spreti, Hans Förstl, and Philipp Martius[51] published their standard work Kunsttherapie bei psychischen Störungen [Art Therapy in Psychological Disorders], I pointed out the profound effectiveness of Painting Therapy, together with Verena Kast's contribution on psychotherapy in mourning crises.

Painting Therapy has found a natural place in

numerous standard works on Jungian psychology, for example in Verena Kast's book The Dynamics of Symbols. Fundamentals of Jungian Psychotherapy,[52] first published in 1990, or in Brigitte Dorst's methodological work Therapeutisches Arbeiten mit Symbolen. Wege in die innere Bilderwelt [Therapeutic Work with Symbols. Paths to the Inner Pictorial Realm].[53] Jung's approach has also found its integral place in standard works, such as Kunsttherapie bei psychischen Störungen [Art Therapy in Psychological Disorders], published by von Spreti, Förstl, and Martius.

Painting Therapy in Practice

In closing, I would like to provide some guidance on the way "painting from the unconscious" is nowadays applied and organized in psychotherapeutic practice.

Current Group Painting Therapy is based on Jolande Jacobi's recommendations insofar as one particular symbol is suggested for joint imagination and painting. In this way, each of the participants may dive deep into the depths of this symbolic field – e.g. the four elements or the basic colors – in order to find their individual experiences and Pictures, which they will then start to elaborate on in a creative manner. As a further step, each of the pictures is jointly contemplated and carefully interpreted together with the group leader.

The therapeutic effectiveness of this form of group therapy is based on the connection of the imagination process, opening up access to the unconscious, with the conscious process of creation that links unconsciously found imaginary symbols with the conscious mind, thereby making them conscious. During the discussion, the artwork – similar to dream interpretation – is united with the concrete life themes of the individual group members. In this process, group members get to know and better understand each other, which in turn enhances the therapeutic effect of this kind of group work.

Individual therapy focusing on "painting from the unconscious" in its current form is also practiced in line with Jung's and Jacobi's concepts, encouraging patients to paint at home on their own – inspired by dream motifs, imaginations, or life themes that have surfaced during therapy sessions and might have even been addressed already – and to then bring their work along to the next therapy session in order for it to be interpreted together with their therapist. As in Jung's days, sometimes a small series of pictures rather than a single picture is discussed because spontaneous changes and developmental steps become more obvious from one picture to the next – both for the creative patients and their therapists. Moreover, a longer and unavoidable interruption in therapy sessions – e.g. during holidays – may be bridged in a useful manner with patients remaining connected with their issues through the painting process.

During dramatic phases of treatment, e.g. if a trauma surfaces and re-manifests itself, encouraging patients to paint during therapy sessions in the practice has proven successful. While painting under the therapist's supervision, patients can be supported and guided in this anxiety-laden situation. Likewise, therapists are in a better position to perceive the processing of the trauma in the symbolic painting process.

At times, painting alongside one another during therapy sessions is a viable option for the patient and the therapist, as it offers the possibility to perceive and possibly complement the nature of a particular symbol or dream Picture by both of them. However, this approach would only be advisable if simultaneous transference processes are recognized on a conscious level.

Notes

[1] *The Red Book. Liber Novus.* Edited and introduced by Sonu Shamdasani. Foreword by Ulrich Hoerni. Introduction, notes of the editor on the edition, annotations and acknowledgements translated from English by Christian Hermes. Philemon Series. 4th edition. Patmos, Ostfildern 2016.

[2] Jacobi, Jolande: *Vom Bilderreich der Seele.* Walter, Zürich/Düsseldorf 1992.

[3] Prinzhorn, Hans: *Artistry of the Mentally Ill.* Springer New York 1972; Morgenthaler, Walter: *Madness and Art: The Life and Works of Adolf Wolfli.* University of Nebraska Press 1992; Pfister, Hans Oskar: Farbe und Bewegung in der Zeichnung Geisteskranker. Aus der Psychiatrischen Universitätsklinik Zürich. In: *Schweizer Archiv für Neurologie und Psychiatrie* 34, 1934, 325-365.

[4] On graphology, cf. Jacobi, Vom Bilderreich der Seele, 25 (with reference to: Helmut, M.: *Menschenkenntnis aus der Handschrift.* Munz, Berlin 1934).

[5] Zimmer, Heinrich: *Myths and Symbols in Indian Art and Civilization.* Princeton University Press, 2017.

[6] Fierz, Karl: Preface. In: Jacobi, *Vom Bilderreich der Seele,* 6.

[7] Jung, C. G., Aims of Psychotherapy (1926). In: *Collected Works* Vol. 16: *Practice of Psychotherapy. Essays on the Psychology of the Transference and Other Subjects.* Bollingen Series XX. Princeton University Press, Princeton NJ 1966. §§ 66-113.

[8] Jung, C. G.: A Study in the Process of Individuation. In: *Collected Works* Vol. 9/I: *Archetypes and the Collective Unconscious.* Princeton University Press, 2nd edition 2014.

[9] Id., CW 16, § 102.

[10] Ibid., § 104.

[11] Ibid., § 106.

[12] Ibid.

[13] Ibid.

[14] Jung, C. G.: Schizophrenia (1958) In: *CW 3: Psychogenesis of Mental Disease.* Princeton University Press, 2nd edition 2014, §§ 553-584.

[15] Jacobi, Vom Bilderreich der Seele, 107: Picture 41: The devouring mother, watercolor and ink, 18-year-old girl.

[16] Cf. ibid., 106-112.

[17] Ibid., 243-277.

[18] Ibid., 243.

[19] Ibid., 247f.

[20] Cf. ibid., 248f.

[21] Ibid., 249.

[22] Ibid.

[23] Ibid., 247.

[24] Picture 181, poster paint, 40-year-old woman, explanations: ibid., 269f.

[25] Ibid., 270.

[26] Picture 183, poster paint, 28-year-old woman, explanations: ibid.

[27] Picture 184, title: "The devilish girl," poster paint, 77-year-old woman, explanations: ibid.

[28] Riedel, Ingrid/Henzler, Christa: *Maltherapie. Auf der Basis der Analytischen Psychologie C. G. Jungs.* Patmos, Ostfildern 2016.

[29] Riedel, Ingrid: *Farben in Religion, Gesellschaft, Kunst und Psychotherapie.* Kreuz, Stuttgart 2008; id.: *Formen. Tiefenpsychologische Deutung von Kreis, Kreuz, Dreieck, Quadrat, Spirale and Mandala.* Kreuz, Stuttgart 2006; id.: *Bilder in Psychotherapie, Kunst und Religion. Ein Schlüssel zur Interpretation.* Kreuz, Stuttgart 2005.

[30] Henzler, Christa/Riedel, Ingrid: *Malen in der Gruppe. Modelle für die therapeutische Arbeit mit Symbolen.* Kreuz, Stuttgart 2008.

[31] Dorst, Brigitte: *Therapeutisches Arbeiten mit Symbolen. Wege in die innere Bilderwelt.* Kohlhammer, Stuttgart 2015.; id.: Der Archetyp der Gruppe. Gruppen als Erfahrungsräume der Individuation und Ko-Individuation. In: *Analytische Psychologie* 181, 3/2015, 336-361.

[32] Bach, Susan R.: Spontanes Malen schwerkranker Patienten. Ein Beitrag zur psychosomatischen Medizin (*Acta Psychosomatica* ; 8). Geigy, Basel 1966; id.: Spontaneous pictures of leukemic children as an expression of the total personality, mind and body. In: *Acta Paedopsychiatry* 41.3, 1975, 86-104; id.: *Das Leben malt seine eigene Wahrheit. Über die Bedeutung spontaner Malereien schwerkranker Kinder.* Daimon, Einsiedeln 1995.

[33] Michel, Rudolf: Studien zur Raumsymbolik (unveröffentlichte Manuskripte). C. G. Jung Institute Zürich.

[34] Bachmann, Helen I.: Malen als Lebensspur. Die Entwicklung kreativer bildlicher Darstellung. *Ein Vergleich mit den frühkindlichen Loslösungs- und Individuationsprozessen.* Klett-Cotta, Stuttgart 1985.

[35] Baumgardt, Ursula: *Kinderzeichnungen – Spiegel der Seele. Kinder zeichnen Konflikte ihrer Familie.* Kreuz, Zürich 1985.

[36] Eschenbach, Ursula (Hg.): Das Symbol im therapeutischen Prozess bei Kindern und Jugendlichen (*Therapeutische Konzepte der analytischen Psychologie C. G. Jungs*; 1). Bonz, Stuttgart 1978; id.: Sinn-Bilder eines Reifungsprozesses weiblicher Identität. In: Pflüger, Peter-Michael (Hg.): *Die Suche nach Sinn heute.* Walter, Olten/Freiburg im Breisgau 1990.

[37] Daniel, Renate: Archetypische Signaturen im unbewussten Malprozeß (*Therapeutische Konzepte der analytischen Psychologie C. G. Jungs*; 6). Bonz, Waiblingen-Hohenacker 1993.

[38] Brutsche, Paul: Zur Bedeutung der Perspektive in Analysanden-Zeichnungen. Diplom-Thesis am C. G. Jung Institut Zürich 1985 (unveröffentlichtes Manuskript).

[39] Krapp, Manfred: Die Gestaltungstherapie als Beitrag zur Psychotherapie der Psychosen. Diplom-Thesis am C. G. Jung Institut Zürich 1986 (unveröffentlichtes Manuskript).

[40] Giera-Krapp, Margitta: Ein Beitrag zur Therapie

der frühen Störungen. Diplom-Thesis am C. G. Jung Institut 1985 (unveröffentlichtes Manuskript).

[41] Benedetti, Gaetano: Psychopathologie und Kunst. In: Condrau, Gion (Hg.): *Transzendenz, Imagination und Kreativität. Religion, Parapsychologie und Kunst* (Die Psychologie des 20. Jahrhunderts; 15) Kindler, Zürich 1979, 1045-1054.

[42] Krapp, Manfred: *Ich-Du-Wir. Zur bildnerischen Symbolik von therapeutischen Transformationsprozessen in Gruppen. Analytische Psychologie und Psychotherapie der Psychosen.* Opus Magnum, Stuttgart 2010.

[43] Clauser, Günter: Die Gestaltungstherapie. Der therapeutische Umgang mit dem schöpferischen Menschen. In: *Praxis der Psychotherapie* 5, 1960, 268-295.

[44] Schottenloher, Gertraud: *Das therapeutische Potential spontanen bildnerischen Gestaltens unter besonderer Berücksichtigung körpertherapeutischer Methoden. Ein integrativer Therapieansatz.* Hartung-Gorre, Konstanz 1989.

[45] Gabriel, Holgrid: Die Behandlung früher Störungen mit kunsttherapeutischen Mitteln aus der Sicht von C. G. Jung. In: Petzold, Hilarion G./Orth, Ilse (Hg.): *Die neuen Kreativitätstherapien. Handbuch der Kunsttherapie. Theorie und Praxis.* Bd. I. Junfermann, Paderborn 1990.

[46] Abt, Theodor: *Introduction to Picture Interpretation According to C. G. Jung.* Living Human Heritage Publ., Zürich 2005.

[47] Henzler, Christa: Aspekte der Maltherapie unter besonderer Berücksichtigung des tiefenpsychologischen Interpretations-Ansatzes. Diplomarbeit an der Universität Kassel 1985 (unveröffentlichtes Manuskript).

[48] Briendl, Linda: Die Wiederbeheimatung in der Welt der Gefühle Kreativität als Ausdruck von Emotion. In: Emrich, Hinderk M./Riedel, Ingrid (Hg.): *Im Farbenkreis der Emotionen. Festschrift für Verena Kast zum 60.* Geburtstag. Königshausen & Neumann, Würzburg 2003, 22-29; id.: *Bilder als Sprache der Seele. Sich selbst entdecken durch Malen und Gestalten.* 2. Aufl. Patmos, Ostfildern 2013.

[49] Henzler, Christa/Riedel, Ingrid: *Malen, um zu überleben. Ein kreativer Weg durch die Trauer.* Kreuz, Stuttgart/Zürich 2003.

[50] Henzler, Christa: Malen gegen den Tod. Die Funktion des Malens bei der Durchschreitung der Trauerphasen. In: *Im Farbenkreis der Emotionen. Festschrift für Verena Kast zum 60.* Geburtstag. Königshausen & Neumann, Würzburg 2003, 54-64.

[51] Spreti, Flora von/Förstl, Hans/Martius, Philipp (Hg.): *Kunsttherapie bei psychischen Störungen,* 2. Aufl. Elsevier, Urban und Fischer, München 2012.

[52] Kast, Verena: *The Dynamics of Symbols. Fundamentals of Jungian Psychotherapy.* Fromm International. 1st American edition 1992.

[53] Dorst, Brigitte: *Therapeutisches Arbeiten mit Symbolen. Wege in die innere Bilderwelt. Kohlhammer,* Stuttgart 2015.

References

Abt, Theodor: *Introduction to Picture Interpretation According to C. G. Jung.* Living Human Heritage Publ., Zürich 2005.

Bach, Susan R.: *Das Leben malt seine eigene Wahrheit. Über die Bedeutung spontaner Malereien schwerkranker Kinder.* Daimon, Einsiedeln 1995.

Bach, Susan R.: Spontaneous pictures of leukemic children as an expression of the total personality, mind and body. In: *Acta Paedopsychiatry* 41.3, 1975.

— —.: Spontanes Malen schwerkranker Patienten.

Ein Beitrag zur psychosomatischen Medizin (*Acta Psychosomatica* 8). Geigy, Basel 1966.

Bachmann, Helen I.: *Malen als Lebensspur. Die Entwicklung kreativer bildlicher Darstellung. Ein Vergleich mit den frühkindlichen Loslösungs- und Individuationsprozessen.* Klett-Cotta, Stuttgart 1985.

Baumgardt, Ursula: *Kinderzeichnungen – Spiegel der Seele. Kinder zeichnen Konflikte ihrer Familie.* Kreuz, Zürich 1985.

Benedetti, Gaetano: Psychopathologie und Kunst. In: Condrau, Gion (Hg.): *Transzendenz, Imagination und Kreativität. Religion, Parapsychologie und Kunst* (Die Psychologie des 20. Jahrhunderts; 15). Kindler, Zürich 1979, 1045-1054.

Briendl, Linda: *Bilder als Sprache der Seele. Sich selbst entdecken durch Malen und Gestalten.* 2. Aufl. Patmos, Ostfildern 2013.

— —.: Die Wiederbeheimatung in der Welt der Gefühle Kreativität als Ausdruck von Emotion. In: Emrich, Hinderk M./ Riedel, Ingrid (Hg.): *Im Farbenkreis der Emotionen. Festschrift für Verena Kast zum 60.* Geburtstag. Königshausen & Neumann, Würzburg 2003, 22-29.

Brutsche, Paul: Zur Bedeutung der Perspektive in Analysanden-Zeichnungen. Diplom-Thesis am C. G. Jung Institut Zürich 1985 (unveröffentlichtes Manuskript).

Clauser, Günter: Die Gestaltungstherapie. Der therapeutische Umgang mit dem schöpferischen Menschen. In: *Praxis der Psychotherapie* 5, 1960, 268-295.

Daniel, Renate: *Archetypische Signaturen im unbewussten Malprozeß (Therapeutische Konzepte der analytischen Psychologie C. G. Jungs*; 6). Bonz, Waiblingen-Hohenacker 1993.

Dorst, Brigitte: Der Archetyp der Gruppe. Gruppen als Erfahrungsräume der Individuation und Ko-Individuation. In: *Analytische Psychologie* 181, 3/2015, 336-361.

— —.: *Therapeutisches Arbeiten mit Symbolen. Wege in die innere Bilderwelt. 2., aktualisierte und erweiterte* Aufl. Kohlhammer, Stuttgart 2015.

Eschenbach, Ursula (Hg.): *Das Symbol im therapeutischen Prozess bei Kindern und Jugendlichen (Therapeutische Konzepte der analytischen Psychologie C. G. Jungs*; 1). Bonz, Stuttgart 1978.

— —.: Sinn-Bilder eines Reifungsprozesses weiblicher Identität. In: Pflüger, Peter-Michael (Hg.): *Die Suche nach Sinn heute.* Walter, Olten/Freiburg im Breisgau 1990.

Gabriel, Holgrid: Die Behandlung früher Störungen mit kunsttherapeutischen Mitteln aus der Sicht von C. G. Jung. In: Petzold, Hilarion G./Orth, Ilse (Hg.): Die neuen Kreativitätstherapien. *Handbuch der Kunsttherapie. Theorie und Praxis.* Bd. I. Junfermann, Paderborn 1990.

Giera-Krapp, Margitta: Ein Beitrag zur Therapie der frühen Störungen. Diplom-Thesis am C. G. Jung Institut 1985 (unveröffentlichtes Manuskript).

Helmut, M.: *Menschenkenntnis aus der Handschrift.* Munz, Berlin 1934.

Jacobi, Jolande: *Vom Bilderreich der Seele.* Walter, Zürich/Düsseldorf 1992.

Henzler, Christa/Riedel, Ingrid: *Malen in der Gruppe. Modelle für die therapeutische Arbeit mit Symbolen.* Kreuz, Stuttgart 2008.

— —./— —.: Malen, um zu überleben. *Ein kreativer Weg durch die Trauer.* Kreuz, Stuttgart/Zürich 2003.

— —.: Aspekte der Maltherapie unter besonderer Berücksichtigung des tiefenpsychologischen Interpretations-Ansatzes. Diplomarbeit an der Universität Kassel 1985 (unveröffentlichtes Manuskript).

— —.: Malen gegen den Tod. Die Funktion des Malens bei der Durchschreitung der Trauerphasen. In: *Im Farbenkreis der Emotionen. Festschrift für Verena Kast zum*

60. Geburtstag. Königshausen & Neumann, Würzburg 2003, 54-64.

Jacobi, Jolande: *Vom Bilderreich der Seele*. Walter, Zürich/Düsseldorf 1992.

Jung, C.G.: *The Red Book*. Liber Novus. Edited and introduced by Sonu Shamdasani. Foreword by Ulrich Hoerni. Introduction, notes of the editor on the edition, annotations and acknowledgements translated from English by Christian Hermes. Philemon Series. 4th edition. Patmos, Ostfildern 2016.

— —.: Schizophrenia (1958) In: CW 3: *Psychogenesis of Mental Disease*. Princeton University Press, 2nd edition 2014.

— —.: Aims of Psychotherapy (1926). In: *Collected Works* Vol. 16: *Practice of Psychotherapy. Essays on the Psychology of the Transference and Other Subjects*. Bollingen Series XX. Princeton University Press, Princeton NJ 1966.

— —.: A Study in the Process of Individuation. In: Collected Works Vol. 9/I: *Archetypes and the Collective Unconscious*. Princeton University Press, 2nd edition 2014.

Kast, Verena: *The Dynamics of Symbols. Fundamentals of Jungian Psychotherapy*. Fromm International. 1st American edition 1992.

Krapp, Manfred: Die Gestaltungstherapie als Beitrag zur Psychotherapie der Psychosen. Diplom-Thesis am C. G. Jung Institut Zürich 1986 (unveröffentlichtes Manuskript).

— —.: Ich-Du-Wir. *Zur bildnerischen Symbolik von therapeutischen Transformationsprozessen in Gruppen. Analytische Psychologie und Psychotherapie der Psychosen*. Opus Magnum, Stuttgart 2010.

Michel, Rudolf: Studien zur Raumsymbolik (unveröffentlichte Manuskripte). C. G. Jung Institute Zürich.

Morgenthaler, Walter: *Madness and Art: The Life and Works of Adolf Wolfli*. University of Nebraska Press 1992.

Pfister, Hans Oskar: Farbe und Bewegung in der Zeichnung Geisteskranker. Aus der Psychiatrischen Universitätsklinik Zürich. In: *Schweizer Archiv für Neurologie und Psychiatrie* 34, 1934.

Prinzhorn, Hans: *Artistry of the Mentally Ill*. Springer New York 1972.

Riedel, Ingrid: *Bilder in Psychotherapie, Kunst und Religion. Ein Schlüssel zur Interpretation*. Kreuz, Stuttgart 2005.

— —.: *Farben in Religion, Gesellschaft, Kunst und Psychotherapie*. Kreuz, Stuttgart 2008.

— —. Formen. *Tiefenpsychologische Deutung von Kreis, Kreuz, Dreieck, Quadrat, Spirale and Mandal*a. Kreuz, Stuttgart 2006.

— —./Henzler, Christa: *Maltherapie. Auf der Basis der Analytischen Psychologie C. G. Jungs*. Patmos, Ostfildern 2016.

Schottenloher, Gertraud: Das therapeutische Potential spontanen bildnerischen Gestaltens unter besonderer Berücksichtigung körpertherapeutischer Methoden. *Ein integrativer Therapieansatz*. Hartung-Gorre, Konstanz 1989.

Spreti, Flora von/Förstl, Hans/Martius, Philipp (Hg.): *Kunsttherapie bei psychischen Störungen*, 2. Aufl. Elsevier, Urban und Fischer, München 2012.

Zimmer, Heinrich: *Myths and Symbols in Indian Art and Civilization*. Princeton University Press, 2017.

CATALOGUES

Thematic Selections from the Archive

In Search of Inner Images

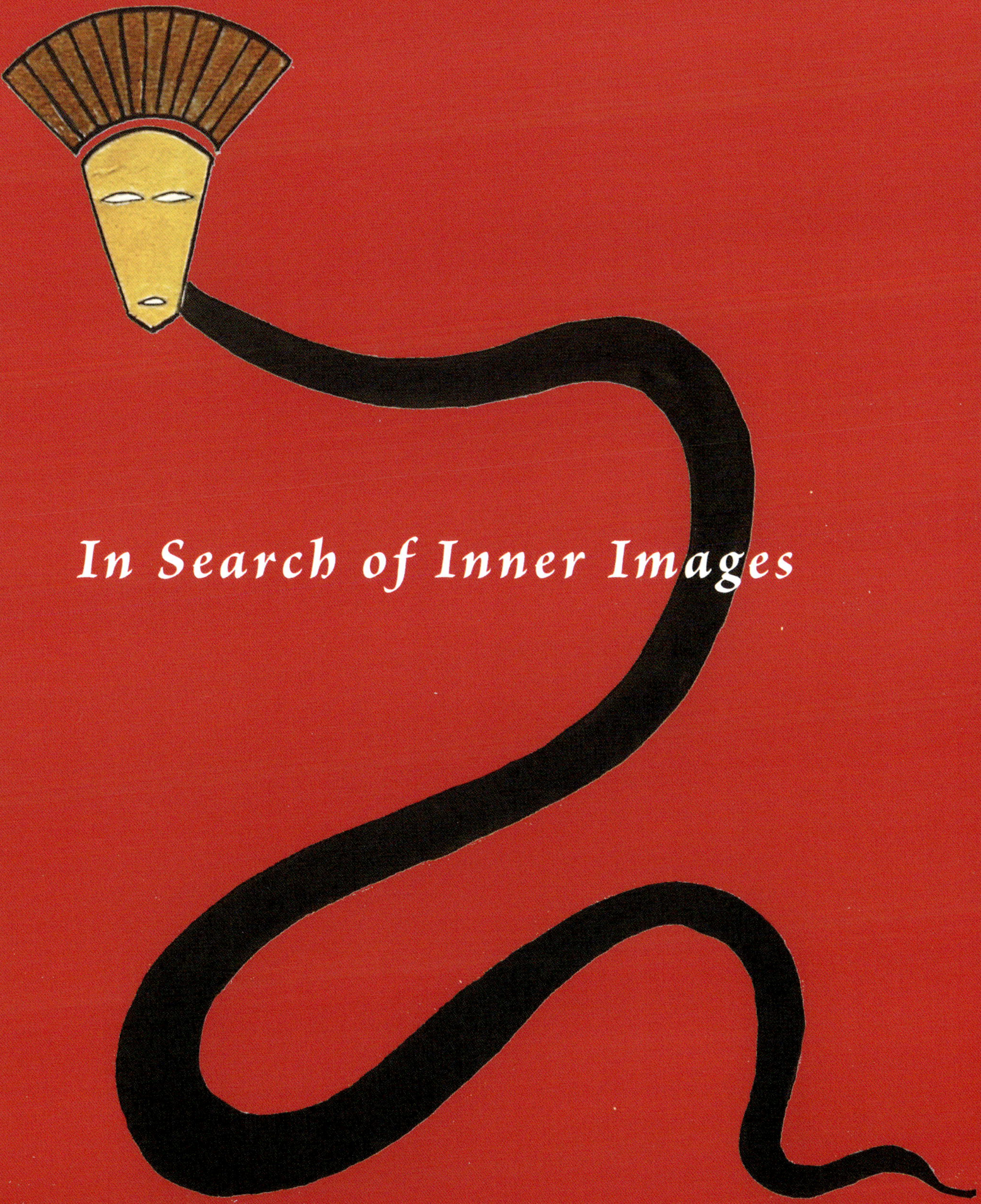

009 AIAA

Anonymous, untitled, 1917
Gouache on paper, 21 × 18 cm

009 AIAB

Anonymous, untitled, 1917
Gouache on paper, 21 × 18 cm

009 AIAD

Anonymous, untitled, 1917
Gouache on paper, 21 × 18 cm

009 AIAF

Anonymous, untitled, 1917
Gouache on paper, 21 × 18 cm

Picture Archive, C.G. Jung Institute Zürich-Küsnacht

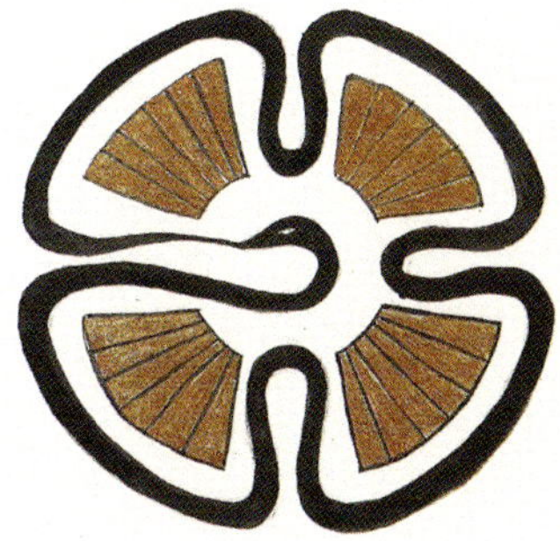

009 AIAG

Anonymous, untitled, 1917
Gouache on paper, 21 × 18 cm

009 AIAI

Anonymous, untitled, 1917
Gouache on paper, 21 × 18 cm

009 AIAJ

Anonymous, untitled, 1917
Gouache on paper, 21 × 18 cm

009 AIAK

Anonymous, untitled, 1917
Gouache on paper, 21 × 18 cm

Picture Archive, C.G. Jung Institute Zürich-Küsnacht

009 AIAL

Anonymous, untitled, 1917
Picture Archive, C.G. Jung Institute Zürich-Küsnacht

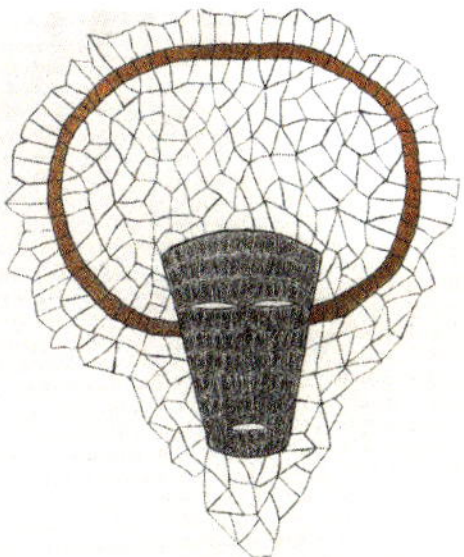
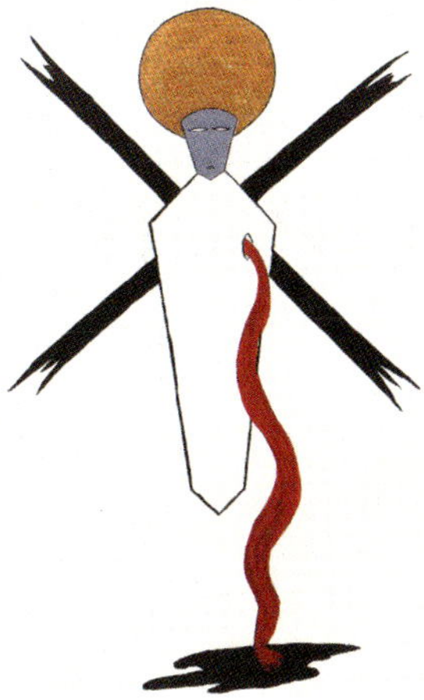
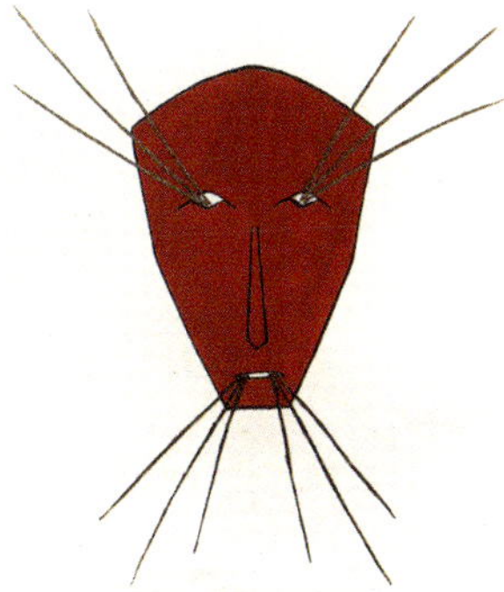

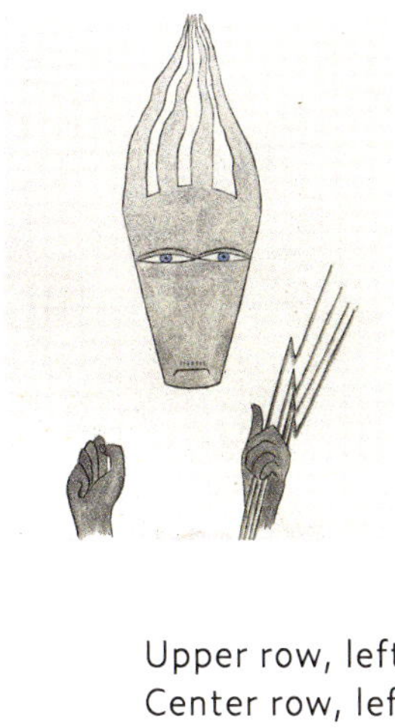

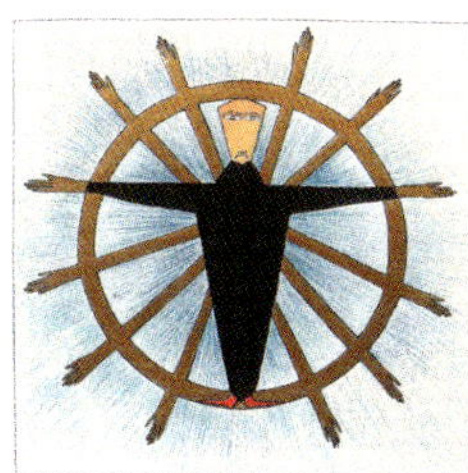
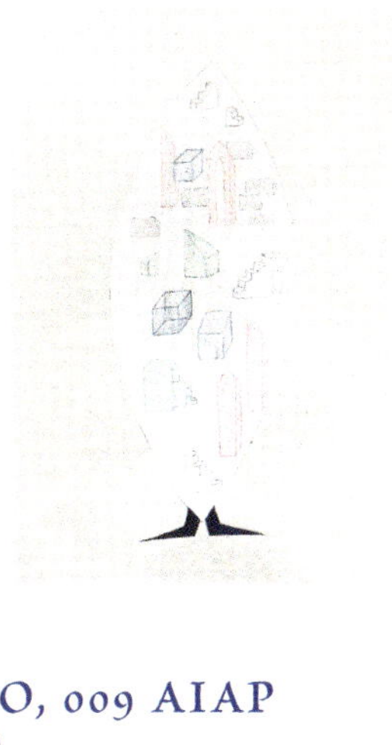

Upper row, left to right: 009 AIAM, 009 AIAN, 009 AIAO, 009 AIAP
Center row, left to right: 009 AIAT, 009 AIAS, 009 AIAQ
Bottom row, left to right: 009 AIBF, 009 AIBB, 009 AIAX, 009 AIBH

All: Anonymous, untitled, 1917/1927/1928
Picture Archive, C.G. Jung Institute Zürich-Küsnacht

009 AIAR

Anonymous, untitled, 1917
Picture Archive, C.G. Jung Institute Zürich-Küsnacht

009 AIAU
Anonymous, untitled, 1917
Picture Archive, C.G. Jung Institute Zürich-Küsnacht

009 AIAV
Anonymous, untitled, 1917
PIcture Archive, C.G. Jung Institute Zürich-Küsnacht

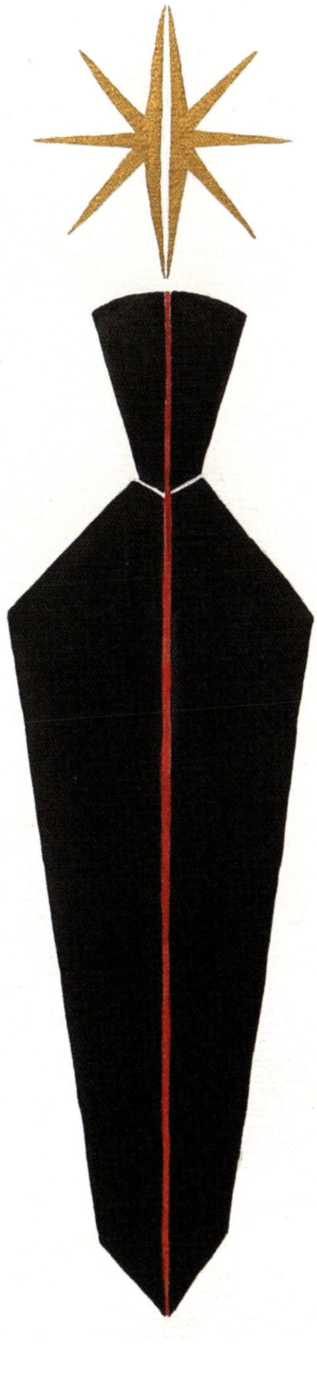

009 AIBA
Anonymous, untitled, 1917
PIcture Archive, C.G. Jung Institute Zürich-Küsnacht

009 AIBD
Anonymous, untitled, 1917
PIcture Archive, C.G. Jung Institute Zürich-Küsnacht

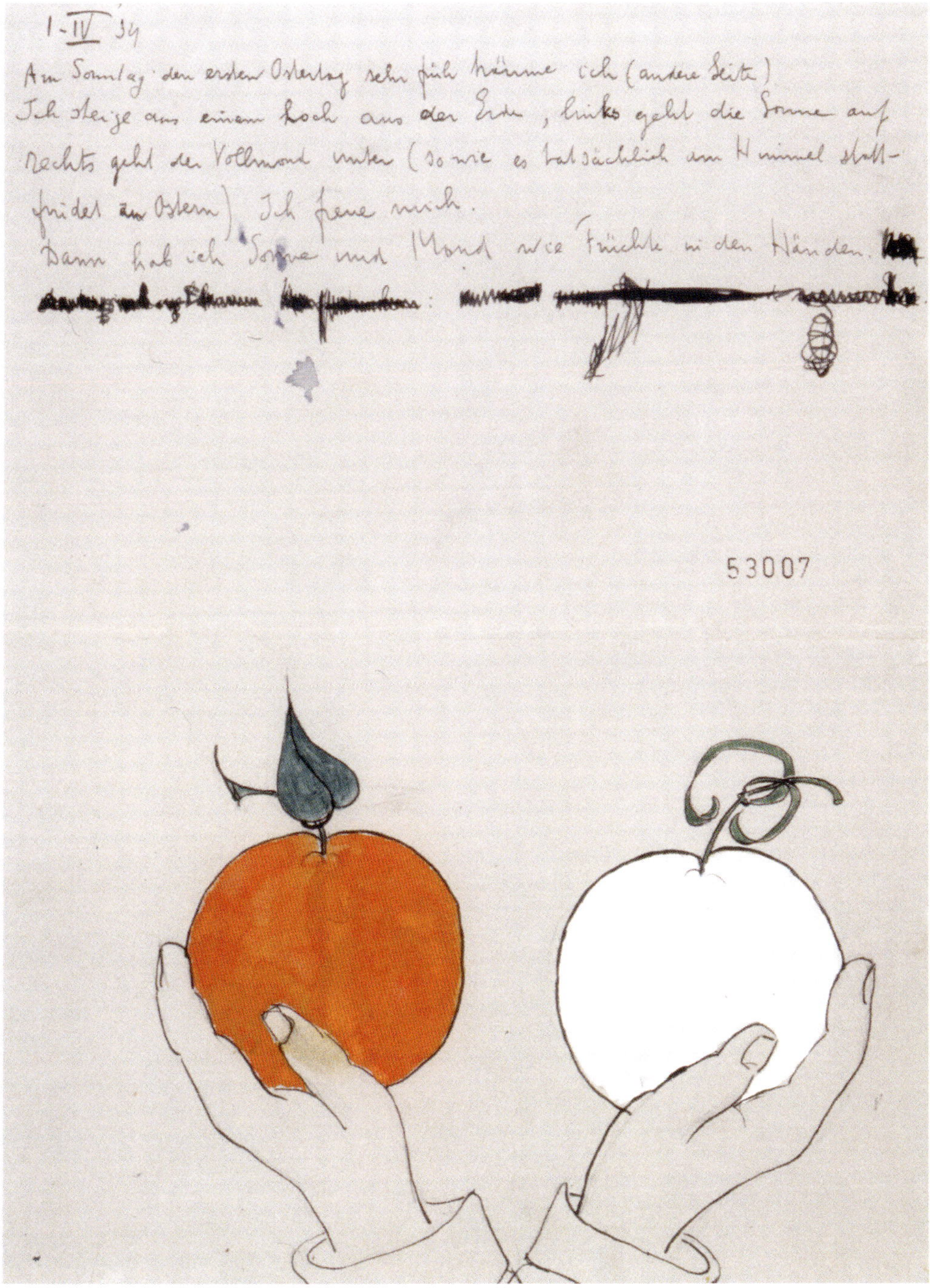

053 CAAD · Anonymous, untitled, 1. 4. 1934
Gouache and ink on paper, 21 × 14 cm
Picture Archive, C.G. Jung Institute Zürich-Küsnacht

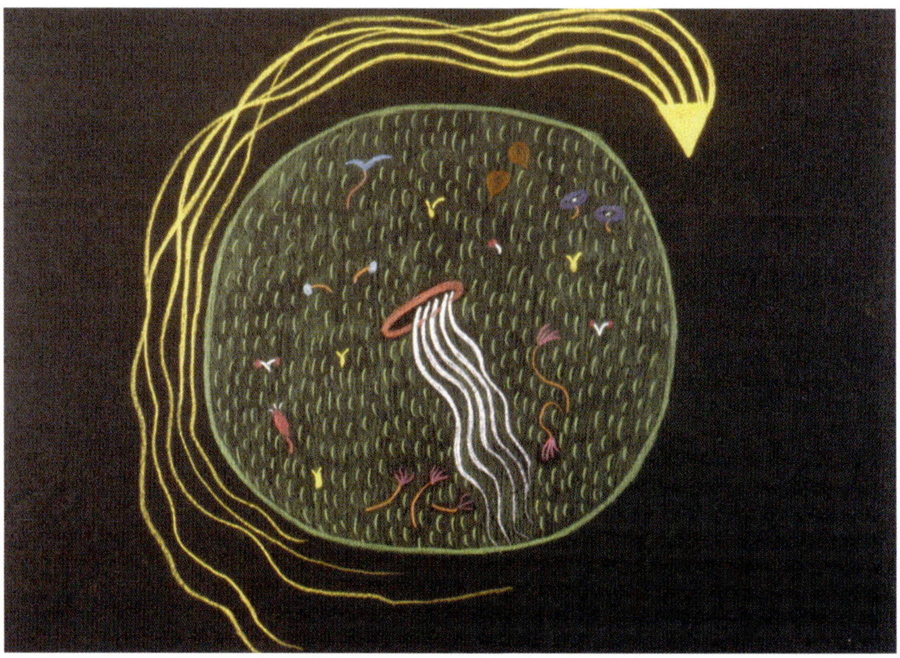

042 BPAM "Das Wunder" ["The Wonder"]

042 BPBA "Gottessehnseucht" ["God's Longing"]
Anonymous, undated, colored pencil on black paper, 31,5 × 46,5 cm.
Picture Archive, C.G. Jung Institute Zürich-Küsnacht

042 BPAO "Bildnis" ["Portrait"]
Anonymous, undated, colored pencil on black paper, 46,5 × 31,5 cm.
Picture Archive, C.G. Jung Institute Zürich-Küsnacht

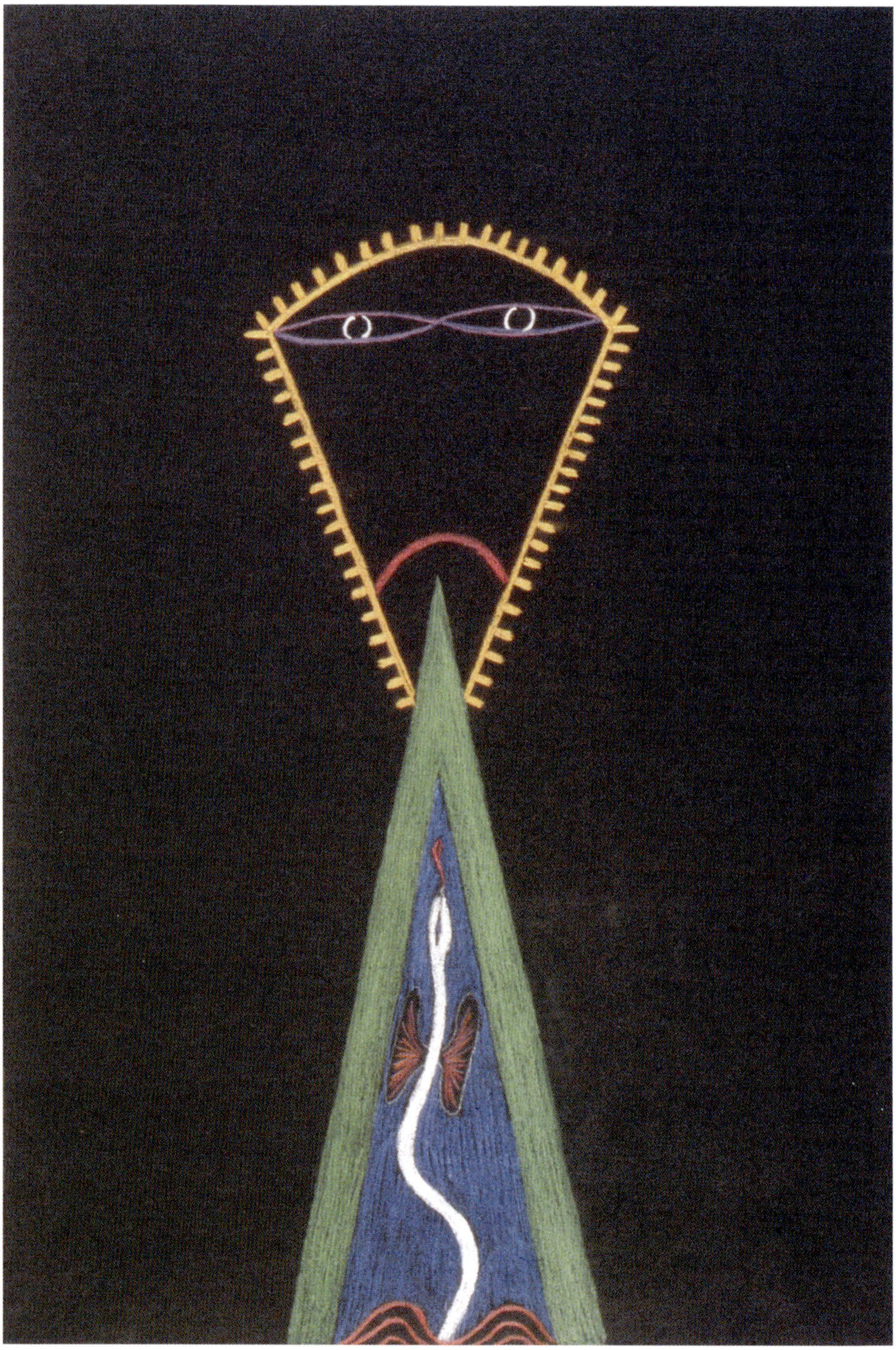

042 BPAU "Gottessehnseucht" ["God's Longing"]
Anonymous, undated, colored pencil on black paper,, 46.5 × 31.5 cm.
Picture Archive, C.G. Jung Institute Zürich-Küsnacht

042 BPBB "Die Erweckung" ["The Resurrection"]
Anonymous, undated, colored pencil on black paper, 45 × 31.5 cm.
Picture Archive, C.G. Jung Institute Zürich-Küsnacht

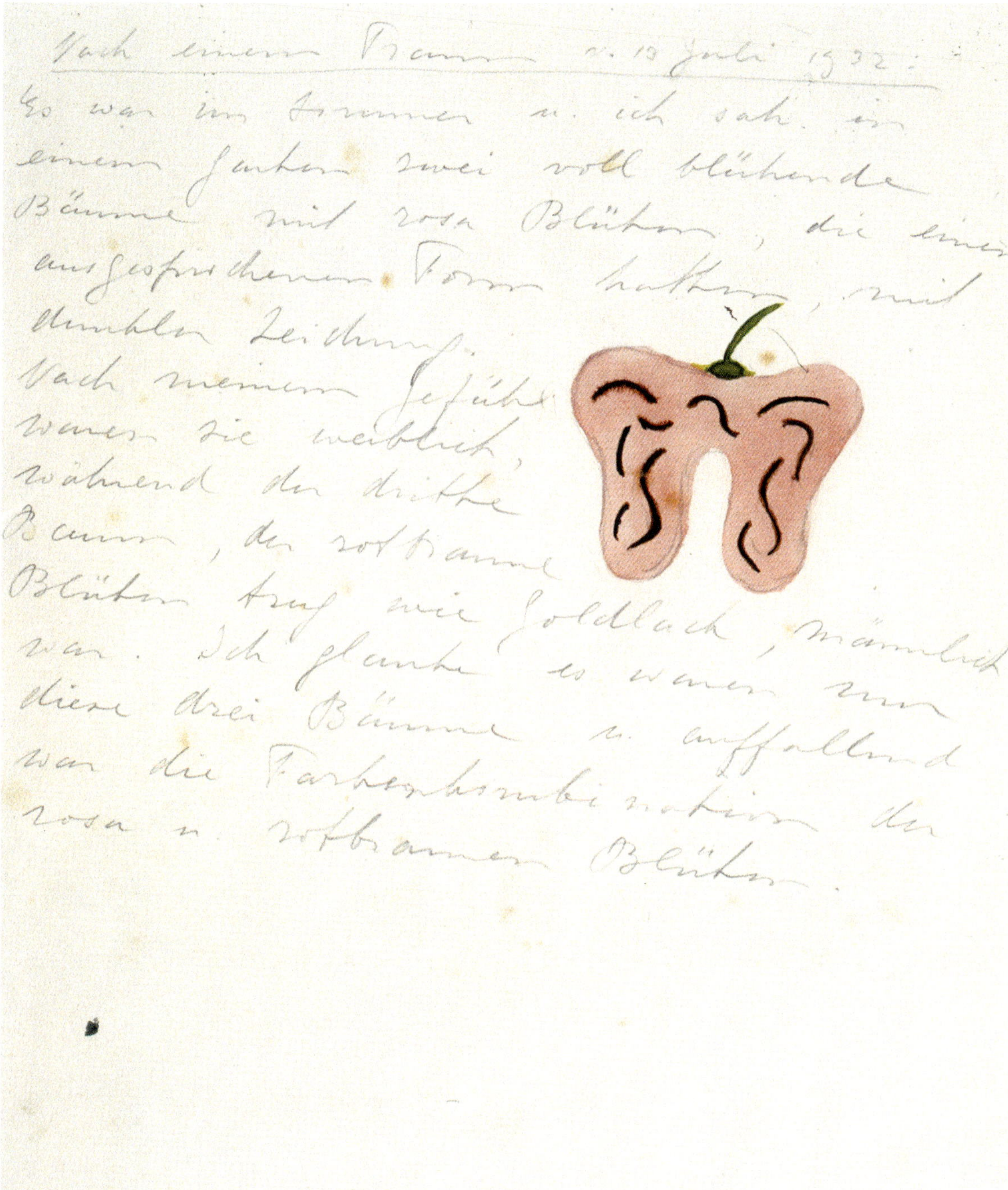

020 ATAK · "Nach einem Traum" ["After a Dream"]
Anonymous, 13. 7. 1932, gouache and ink on paper, 25 × 20 cm.
Picture Archive, C.G. Jung Institute Zürich-Küsnacht

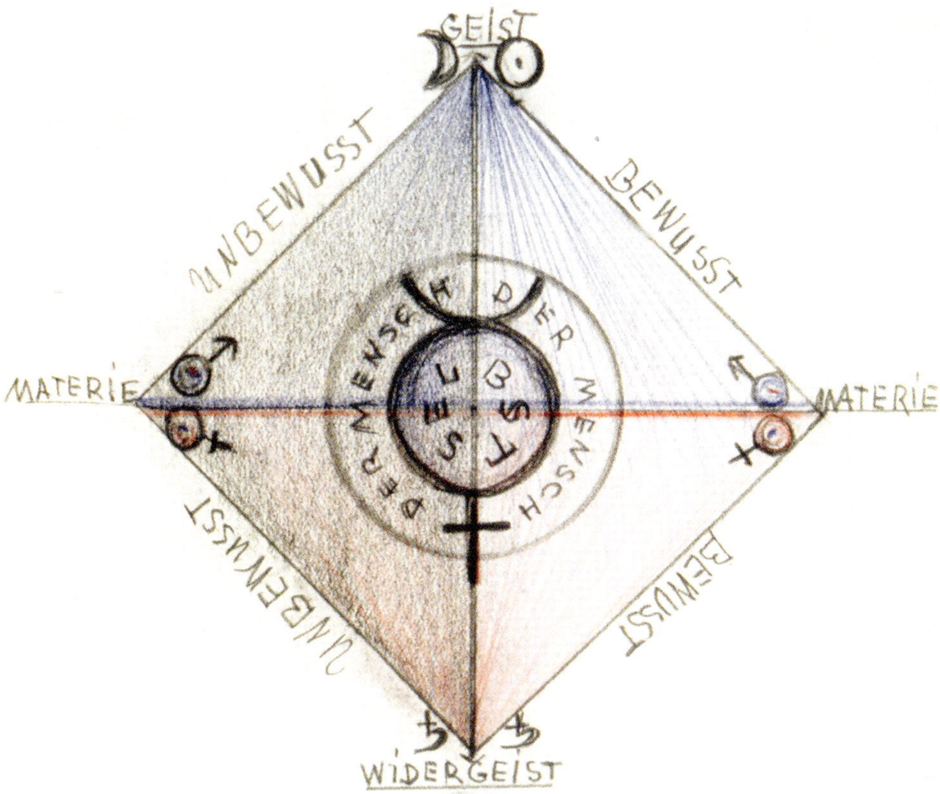

077 CYCB "Ein Tag wie alle" ["A Day like All the Others"]
Anonymous, 20. 11. 1938, gouache on paper, 26.5 × 14.5 cm.
PIcture Archive, C.G. Jung Institute Zürich-Küsnacht

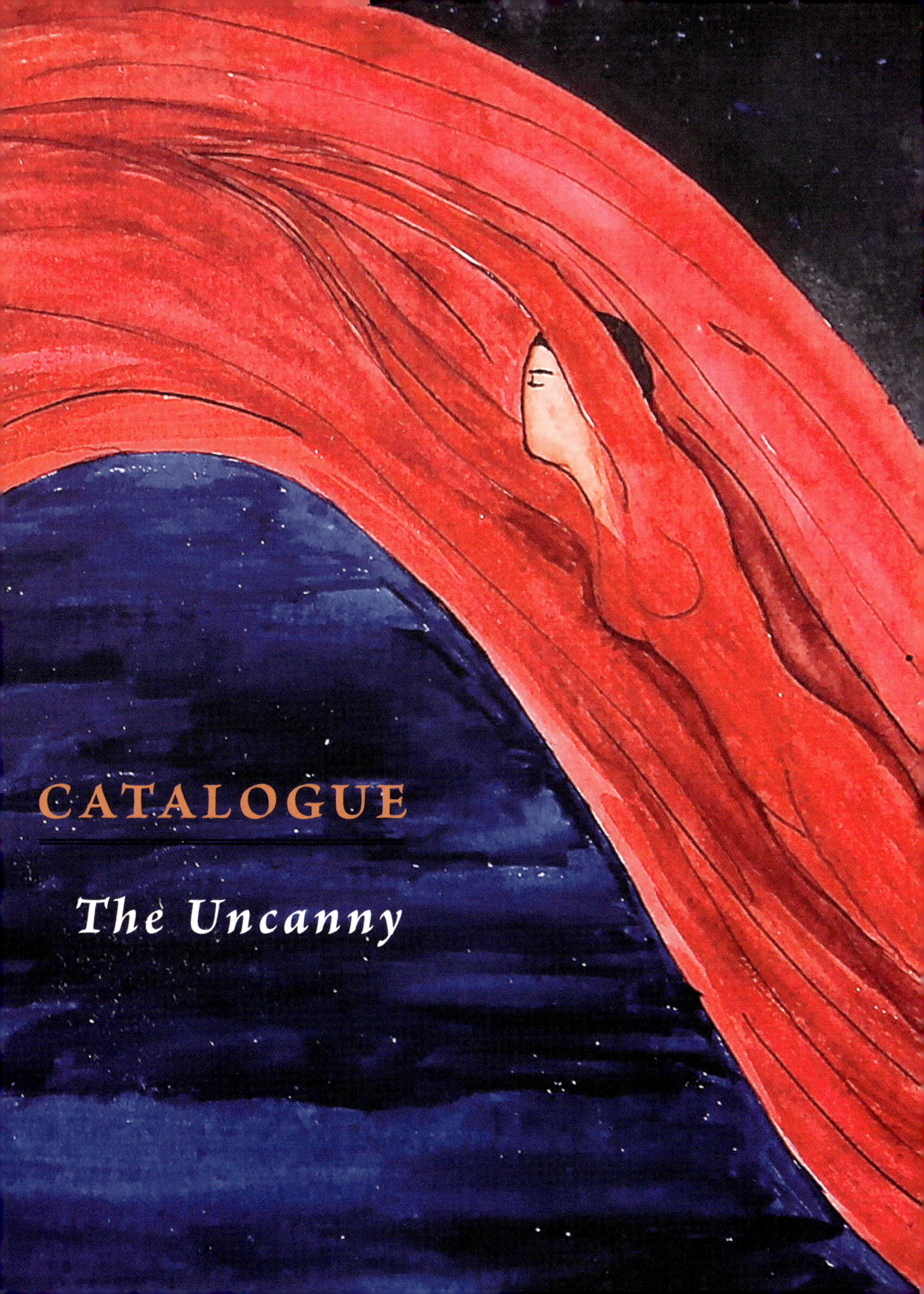

CATALOGUE

The Uncanny

001 AAAA · Anonymous, untitled, 1933
Gouache on paper, 22.5 × 14 cm
Picture Archive of the C.G. Jung Institute Zürich-Küsnacht

001 AAAB · Anonymous, untitled, 24. 10. 1933
Gouache on paper, 22.5 × 14 cm
Picture Archive of the C.G. Jung Institute Zürich-Küsnacht

001 AAAC • Anonymous, untitled, 1933
Gouache on paper, 22.5 × 14 cm
Picture Archive of the C.G. Jung Institute Zürich-Küsnacht

025 AYAK • Anonymous, untitled, undated
Crayon on paper, 30.5 × 23.5 cm
Picture Archive of the C.G. Jung Institute Zürich-Küsnacht

105 EAKR • Anonymous, untitled, 4 October [no year]
Crayon on paper, 22 × 14 cm
Picture Archive of the C.G. Jung Institute Zürich-Küsnacht

105 EATT • Anonymous, untitled, undated
Crayon on paper, 30.5 × 23.5 cm
Picture Archive of the C.G. Jung Institute Zürich-Küsnacht

CATALOGUE

Mandalas

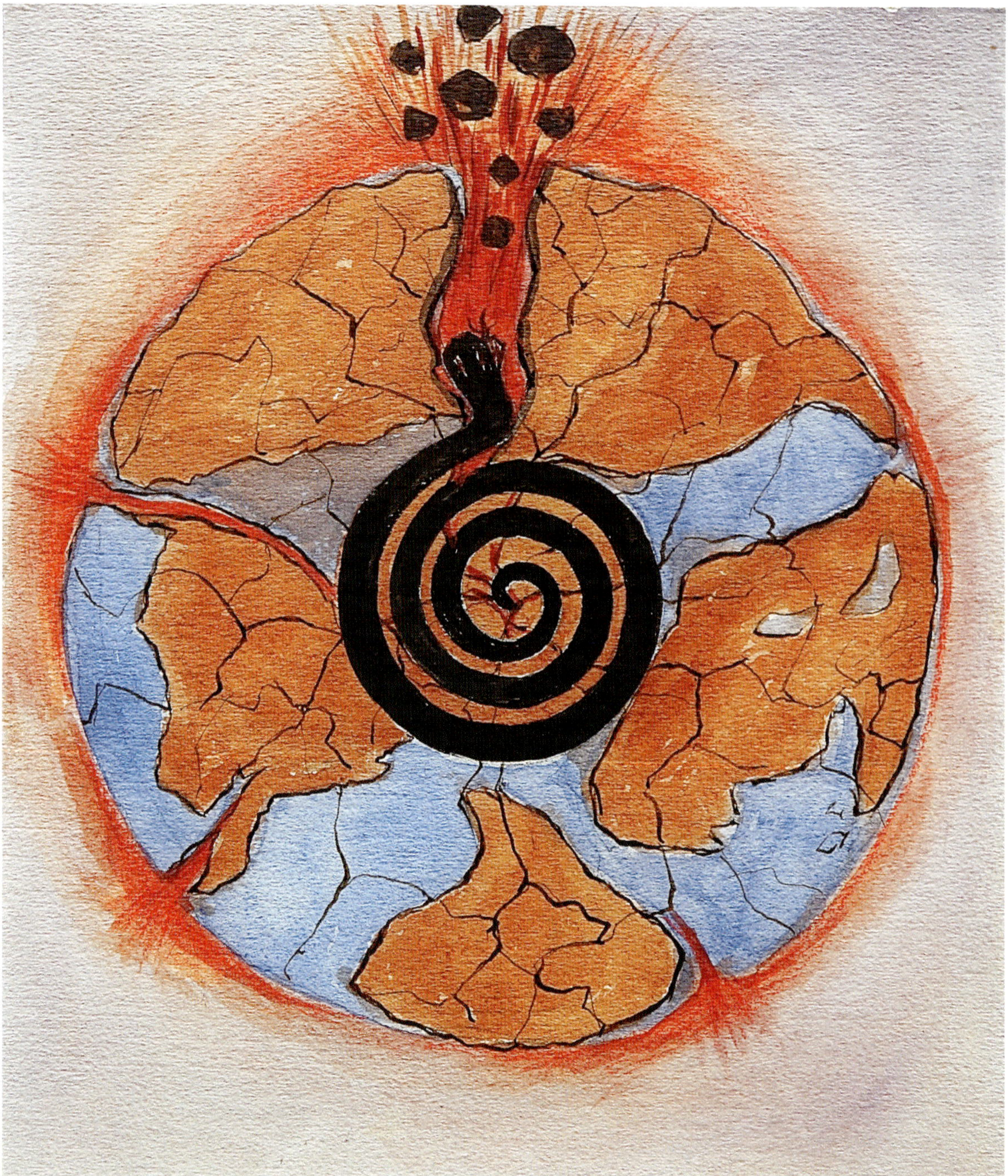

002 ABBH Anonymous, no title
Gouache on paper 22 × 19 cm, 1934.
Picture Archive, C.G. Jung Institute Zürich-Küsnacht

025 AYBC Anonymous, untitled, undated
Gouache on on Paper, 14 x 14 cm
Picture Archive, C.G. Jung Institute Zürich-Küsnacht

002 ABAC "Bunte Sonne" ["Colorful Sun"]
Anonymous, colored pencil on paper, 15 x 17 cm, 1931
Picture Archive, C.G. Jung Institute Zürich-Küsnacht

105 EACB Anonymous, untitled, undated
Pastel on paper, 22.5 × 24.5 cm
Picture Archive, C.G. Jung Institute Zürich-Küsnacht

105 EAGA Anonymous, untitled, undated
Pastel on paper, 21 × 30 cm
Picture Archive, C.G. Jung Institute Zürich-Küsnacht

105 EATD Anonymous, untitled, undated
Gouache on paper, 22.5 × 30 cm
Picture Archive, C.G. Jung Institute Zürich-Küsnacht

039 BMAX Anonymous, untitled,(text on reverse), 1928
Gouache on paper, 28.5 × 22.5 cm
Picture Archive, C.G. Jung Institute Zürich-Küsnacht

065 CMAB Anonymous, untitled, 17. 8. 1935
Gouache on paper, 31.5 × 49.5 cm
Picture Archive, C.G. Jung Institute Zürich-Küsnacht

065 CMAC Anonymous, untitled, 27. 8. 1935
Gouache on paper, 31.5 × 49.5 cm
Picture Archive, C.G. Jung Institute Zürich-Küsnacht

074 CVBB Anonymous, untitled, 7. 8. 1948
Gouache on paper, 33 × 25 cm
Picture Archive, C.G. Jung Institute Zürich-Küsnacht

076 CXFV Anonymous, untitled, 5. 1. 1941
Watercolor on paper, 30 × 21.5 cm
Picture Archive, C.G. Jung Institute Zürich-Küsnacht

076 CXCU Anonymous, untitled, 24. 8. 1939
Gouache on paper, 21.5 × 30 cm
Picture Archive, C.G. Jung Institute Zürich-Küsnacht

016 APBH · "Black Forces" ("Schwarze Kräfte") Anonymous, 1. 11. 1931
Gouache on paper, 25 × 35 cm
Picture Archive, C.G. Jung Institute Zürich-Küsnacht

016 APCN · "The Light of the Body (Das Licht des Körpers)
Anonymous, 30. 12. 1942. Gouache on paper, 22 × 26.5 cm
Picture Archive, C.G. Jung Institute Zürich-Küsnacht

016 APCT · Anonymous, untitled, 29. 8. 1943
Gouache on paper, 22 × 26.5 cm
Picture Archive, C.G. Jung Institute Zürich-Küsnacht

016 APCU · Anonymous, untitled, 20. 1. 1944
Gouache on paper, 22 × 27 cm
Picture Archive, C.G. Jung Institute Zürich-Küsnacht

044 CVAN · "Dream, 9. August," Anonymous, 5. 12. 1934
Gouache on paper, 33 × 25 cm
Picture Archive, C.G. Jung Institute Zürich-Küsnacht

077 CYAT · "Die psychische Totalität" [The Entire Psyche]
Anonymous,, 8. 11. 1938. Crayon on paper, 14.5 × 10.5 cm
Picture Archive, C.G. Jung Institute Zürich-Küsnacht

001 AABC · Anonymous, untitled, 23. 2. 1939
Gouache on paper, 2.5 × 21 cm
Picture Archive, C.G. Jung Institute Zürich-Küsnacht

023 AWAE · "Kundalini"Anonymous, 23. 7. 1929
Gouache on paper, 36 × 24.5 cm
Picture Archive, C.G. Jung Institute Zürich-Küsnacht

037 BKAH · Anonymous, untitled, undated
Gouache on paper (Heft), 30 × 21.5 cm
Picture Archive, C.G. Jung Institute Zürich-Küsnacht

037 BKAM · Anonymous, untitled, undated
Gouache on paper (Heft), 21.5 × 30 cm
Picture Archive, C.G. Jung Institute Zürich-Küsnacht

019 ASBE · Anonymous, untitled, undated
Gouache on paper, 36 × 22 cm
Picture Archive, C.G. Jung Institute Zürich-Küsnacht

019 ASBF · Anonymous, untitled, undated
Gouache on paper, 36 × 22 cm
Picture Archive, C.G. Jung Institute Zürich-Küsnacht

003 ACAB · Anonymous, untitled, 1936
Gouache on paper, 30.5 × 23 cm
Picture Archive, C.G. Jung Institute Zürich-Küsnacht

099 DUCP · Anonymous, untitled, 23..6. o. J
Gouache on paper, 21.5 × 30 cm
Picture Archive, C.G. Jung Institute Zürich-Küsnacht

027 BAAX · Anonymous, untitled, 1932
Colored pencil on paper, 21.5 × 30 cm
Picture Archive, C.G. Jung Institute Zürich-Küsnacht

058 CFAJ · "Der Schlangenweg der 4. Funktionen. Zeit – Weg – Bahn
Anonymous, undated, colored pencil on paper, 27.5 × 21 cm
Picture Archive, C.G. Jung Institute Zürich-Küsnacht

020 ATAJ · Anonymous, "refers to a dream of 13. 7. 1932", undated
Gouache on paper, 25 × 20 cm
Picture Archive, C.G. Jung Institute Zürich-Küsnacht

008 ABAC · "The Hatching of the Egg"
February 10, 1927. Gouache on paper, 16.5 x 16.5 cm

008 AHAF · Untitled, March 17, 1927
Gouache on paper, 20.5 x 20.5 cm

008 AHAD
"The First Tree of Life from the Egg,"
Gouache on paper, 31 x 21 cm
Picture Archive, C.G. Jung Institute Zürich-Küsnacht

These three paintings by the same anonymous patient are discussed in the chapter by Verena Kast.

024 AXAM · Anonymous, untitled, undated
Gouache on paper, 30 × 20 cm
Picture Archive, C.G. Jung Institute Zürich-Küsnacht

CATALOGUE

Sexuality and the Body

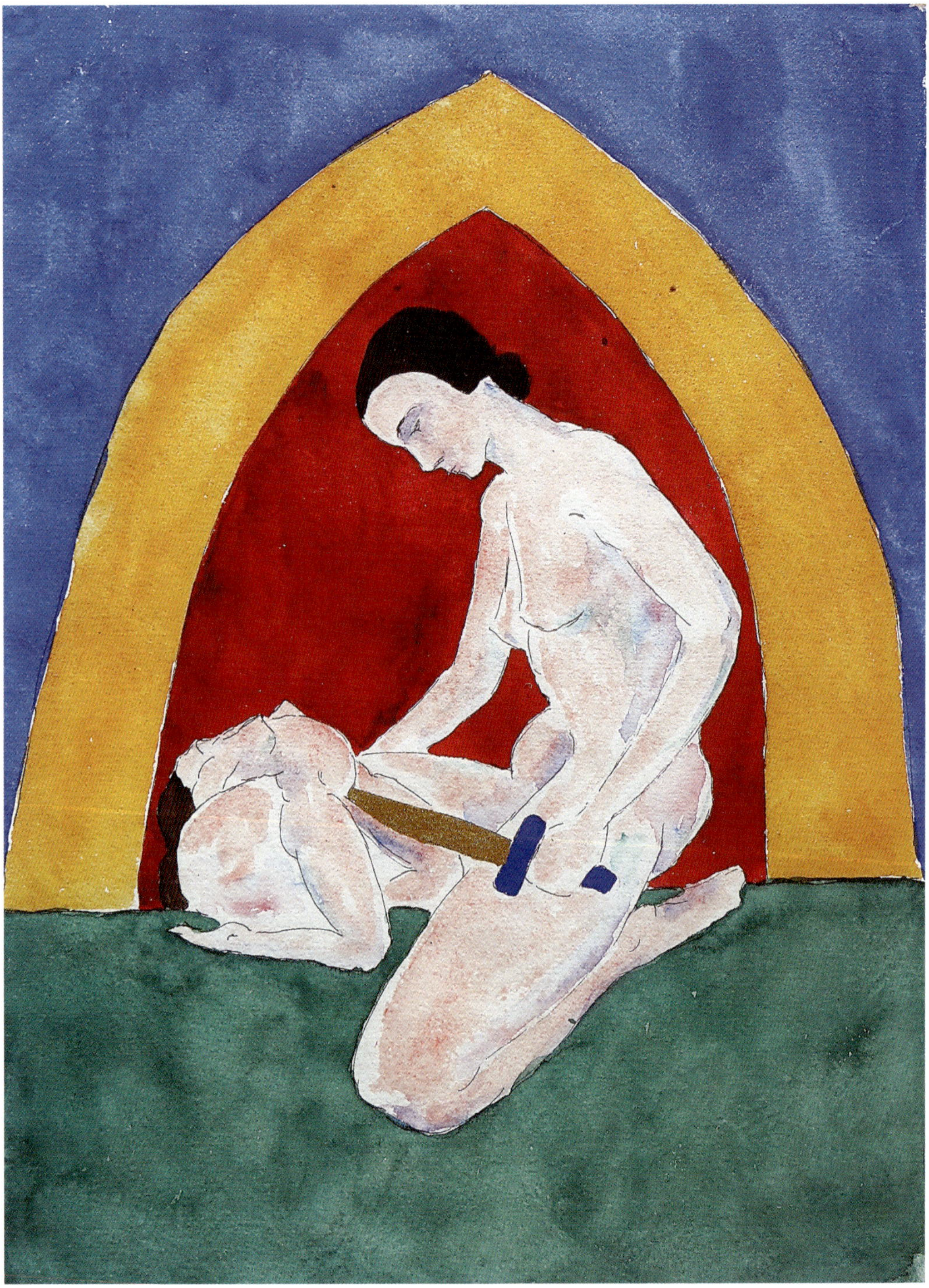

003 ACAM

Anonymous, untitled, 1936, gouache on paper, 30 × 23 cm
Picture Archive, C.G. Jung Institute Zürich-Küsnacht

003 ACAN

Anonymous, untitled, 1936, gouache on paper, 30 × 23 cm
Picture Archive, C.G. Jung Institute Zürich-Küsnacht

105 EAUN

Anonymous, untitled, 30 December 1934 – 1 January 1935, gouache on paper, 24 × 30 cm
Picture Archive, C.G. Jung Institute Zürich-Küsnacht

105 EAUO

Anonymous, untitled, undated, gouache on paper, 24 × 30 cm
Picture Archive, C.G. Jung Institute Zürich-Küsnacht

105 EAVG
Anonymous, untitled, 19 February 1935, gouache on paper, 21.5 × 30,5 cm
Picture Archive, C.G. Jung Institute Zürich-Küsnacht

105 EBEB
Anonymous, untitled, undated, gouache on paper, 22 × 29 cm
Picture Archive, C.G. Jung Institute Zürich-Küsnacht

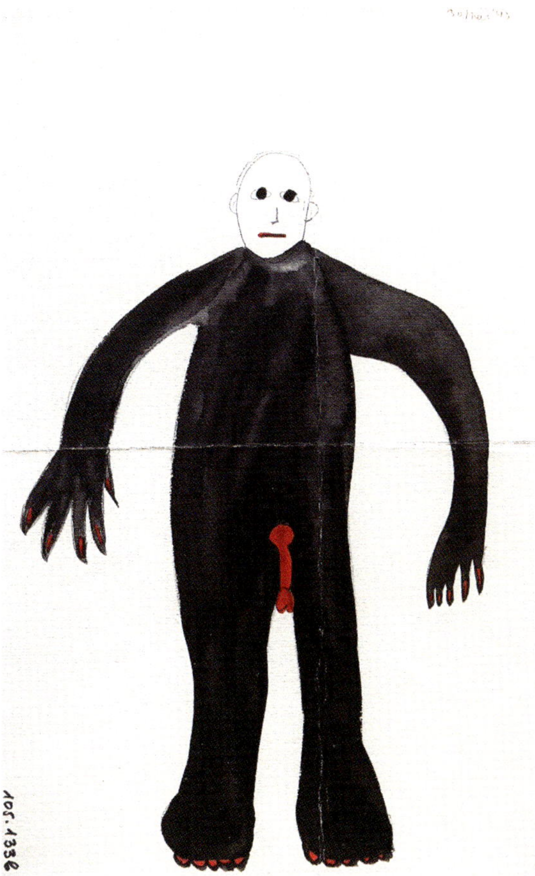

005 EBJO
Anonymous, untitled, 30 March 1945, gouache on paper, 30 × 22 cm
Picture Archive, C.G. Jung Institute Zürich-Küsnacht

105 EBMK
Anonymous, untitled, 21 December 1946, gouache on paper, 15 × 9.5 cm
Picture Archive, C.G. Jung Institute Zürich-Küsnacht

056 CDAB

Anonymous, untitled, undated, watercolor on paper, 23 × 17.5 cm
Picture Archive, C.G. Jung Institute Zürich-Küsnacht

055 CCAB

Anonymous, untitled, undated, gouache on paper, 29 × 21.5 cm
Picture Archive, C.G. Jung Institute Zürich-Küsnacht

064 CLAC

Anonymous, "Analysis," undated, photograph of a watercolor, , 13 × 18 cm
Picture Archive, C.G. Jung Institute Zürich-Küsnacht

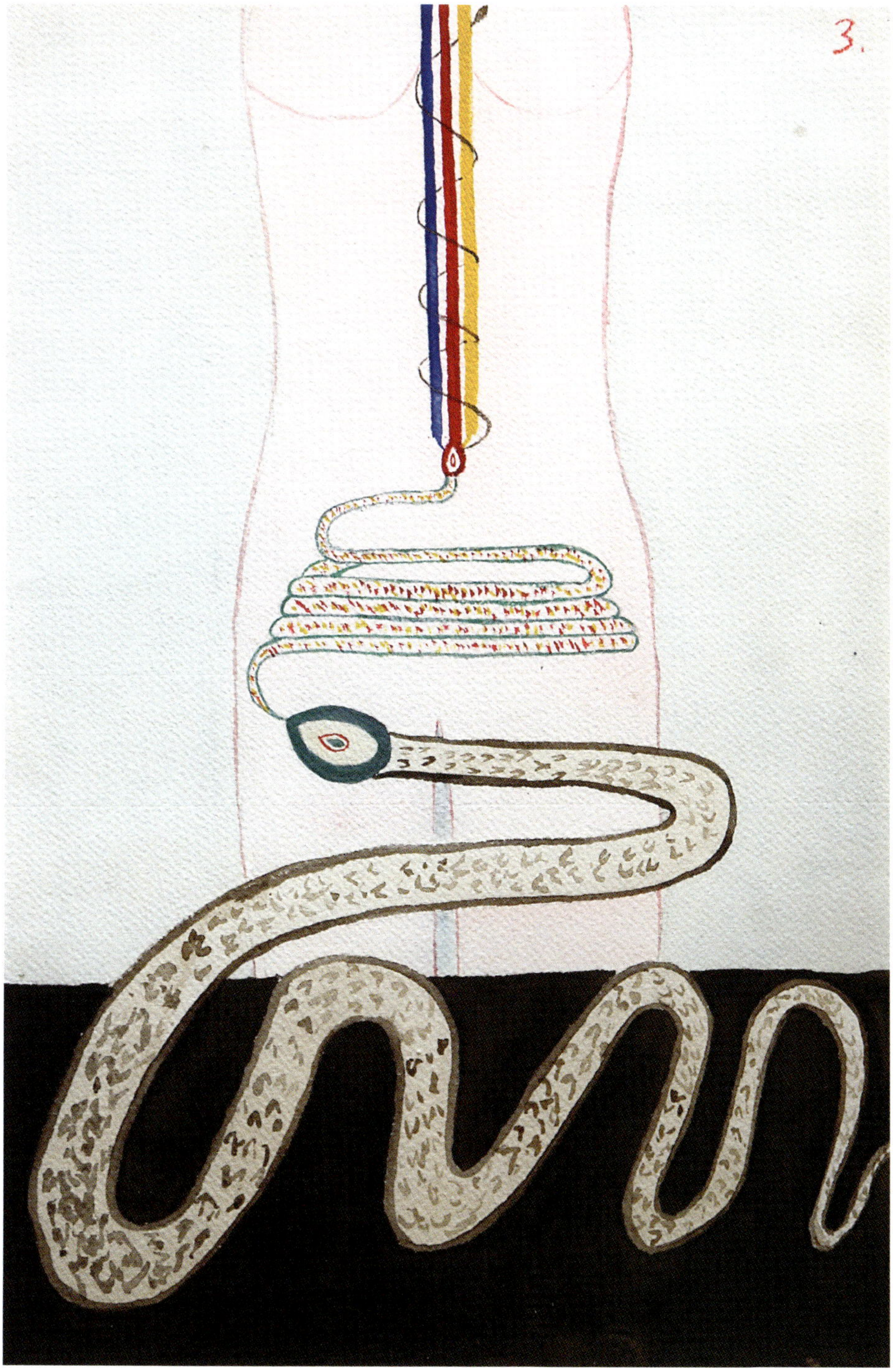

028 BBAC

Anonymous, untitled, November 1928, gouache on paper, 31 × 21 cm
Picture Archive, C.G. Jung Institute Zürich-Küsnacht

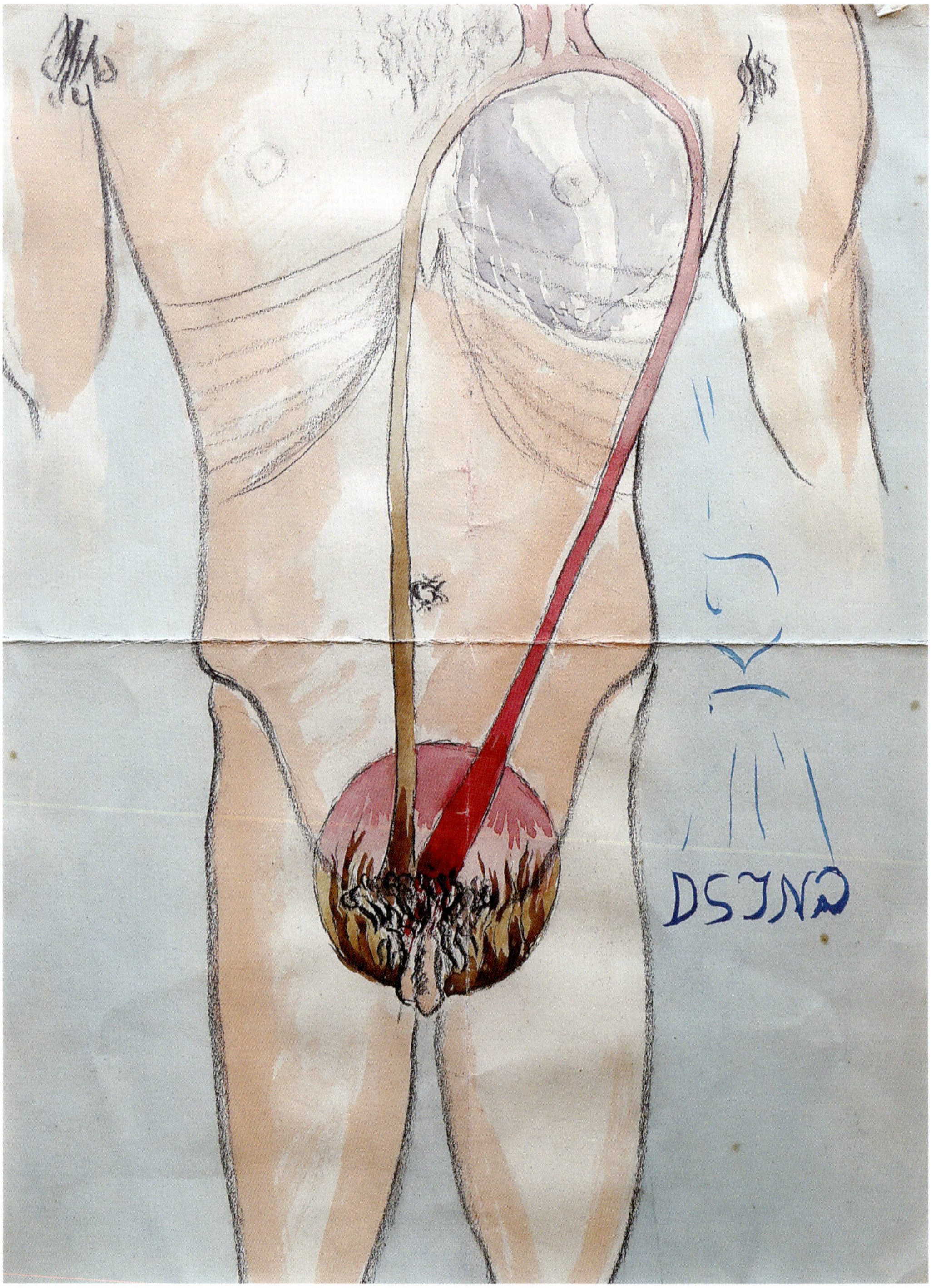

061 CIAB

Anonymous, untitled, undated, gouache and pencil on paper, 36 × 26.5 cm
Picture Archive, C.G. Jung Institute Zürich-Küsnacht

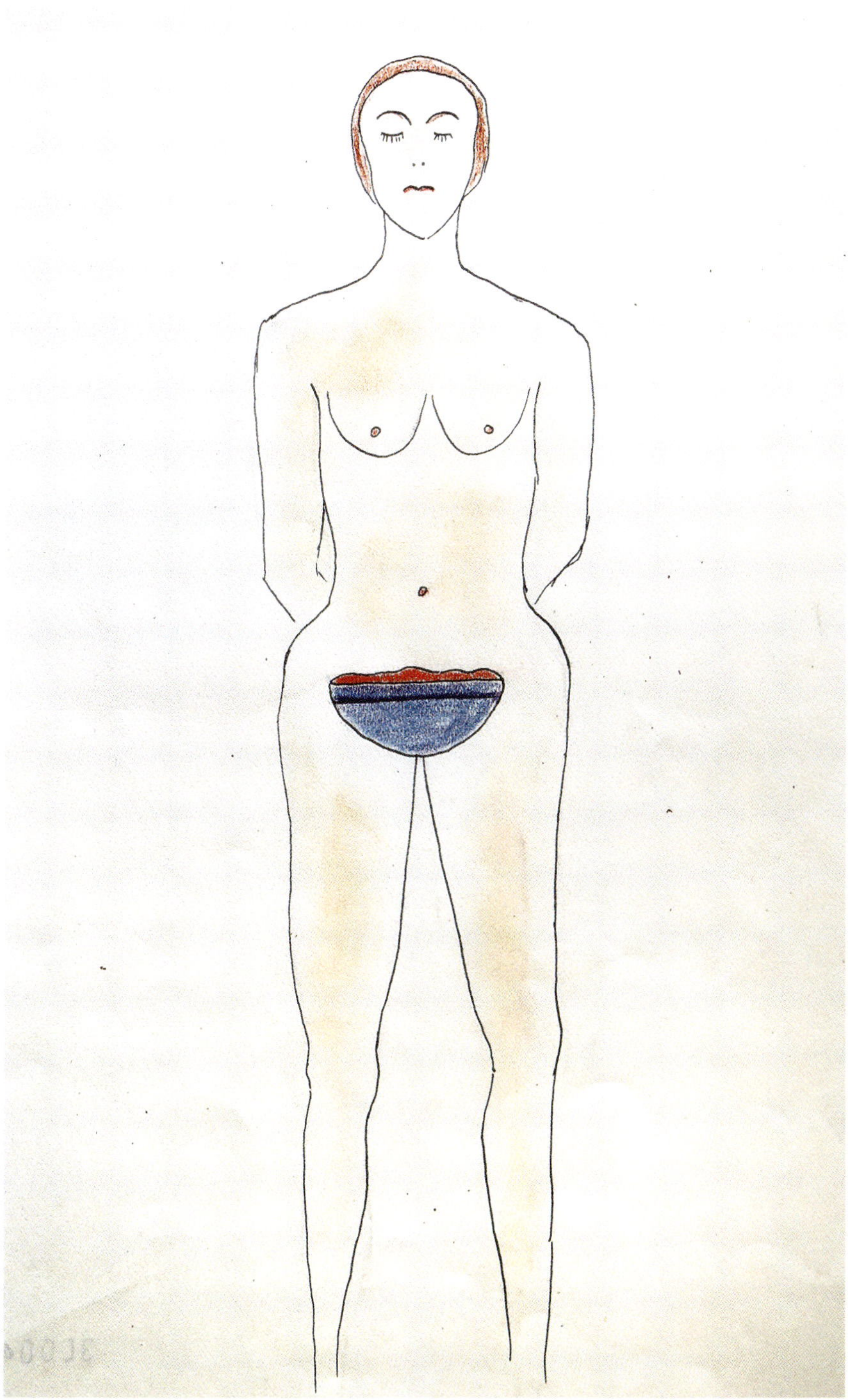

030 BDAD

Anonymous, untitled, undated, pencil and crayon on paper, 29,5 × 20,5 cm
Picture Archive, C.G. Jung Institute Zürich-Küsnacht

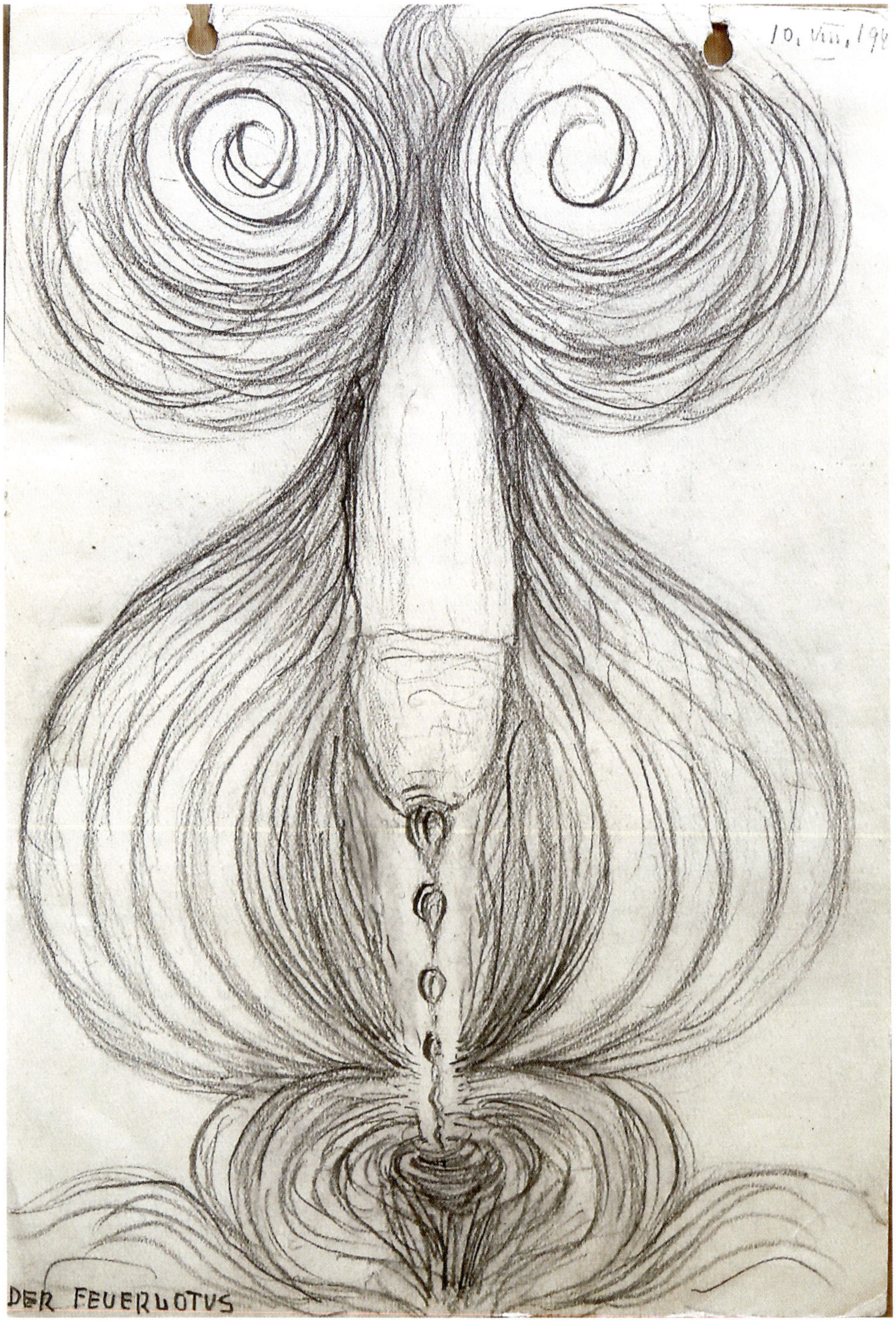

077 CYDM "Der Feuerlotus" ["The Firelotus"]
Anonymous, 10. 8. 1940. pencil on paper, 21 × 14,5 cm
Picture Archive, C.G. Jung Institute Zürich-Küsnacht

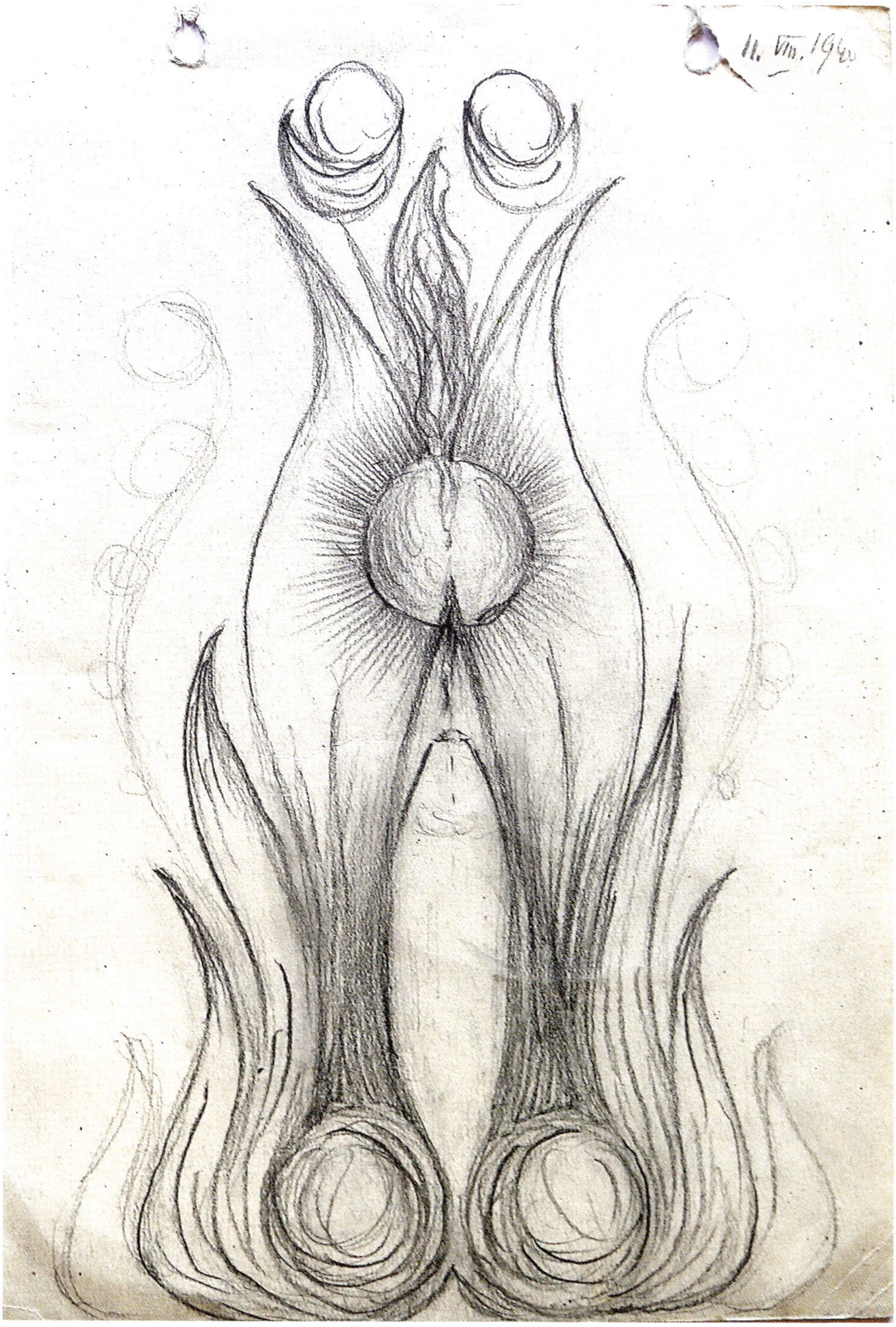

077 CYDN

Anonymous, untitled, 11. 8. 1940, pencil on paper, 21 × 14,5 cm
Picture Archive, C.G. Jung Institute Zürich-Küsnacht

026 AEAM "Oktopus and Mutter" ["Octopus and Mother"]
Anonymous, undated, pencil on paper, 24.5 × 32 cm
Picture Archive, C.G. Jung Institute Zürich-Küsnacht

034 BHAQ "De Leviatan sterft gelijk met Christus" ("Der Leviatan stirbt so wie Christus")
Anonymous, undated, charcoal on paper, 58,5 × 5.,5 cm
Picture Archive, C.G. Jung Institute Zürich., Küsnacht

034 BHAU "Die schwarze Madonna" ["The Black Madonna"]
Anonymous, undated, coal on paper, 58.5 × 53.5 cm
Picture Archive, C.G. Jung Institute Zürich-Küsnacht

034 BHAW
Anonymous, untitled, undated, charcoal on paper, 58.5 × 53.5 cm
Picture Archive, C.G. Jung Institute Zürich-Küsnacht

002 ABAM

Anonymous, untitled, 22. 9. 1934, gouache on paper, 27 × 20 cm
Picture Archive, C.G. Jung Institute Zürich-Küsnacht

002 ABAP

Anonymous, untitled, 2. 10. 1934, gouache on paper, 19,5 × 13 cm
Picture Archive, C.G. Jung Institute Zürich-Küsnacht

002 ABFC

Anonymous, untitled, 27. 7. 1935, gouache on paper, 23 × 18 cm
Picture Archive, C.G. Jung Institute Zürich-Küsnacht

002 ABFD

Anonymous, untitled, 27. 7. 1935, gouache on paper, 23 × 18 cm
Picture Archive, C.G. Jung Institute Zürich-Küsnacht

002 ABGN

Anonymous, untitled, 25. 4. 1936, gouache on paper, 22.5 × 18 cm
Picture Archive, C.G. Jung Institute Zürich-Küsnacht

002 ABGO

Anonymous, untitled, 12. 5. 1936, gouache on paper, 23 × 18 cm
Picture Archive, C.G. Jung Institute Zürich-Küsnacht

CATALOGUE

Tribulations and Destruction

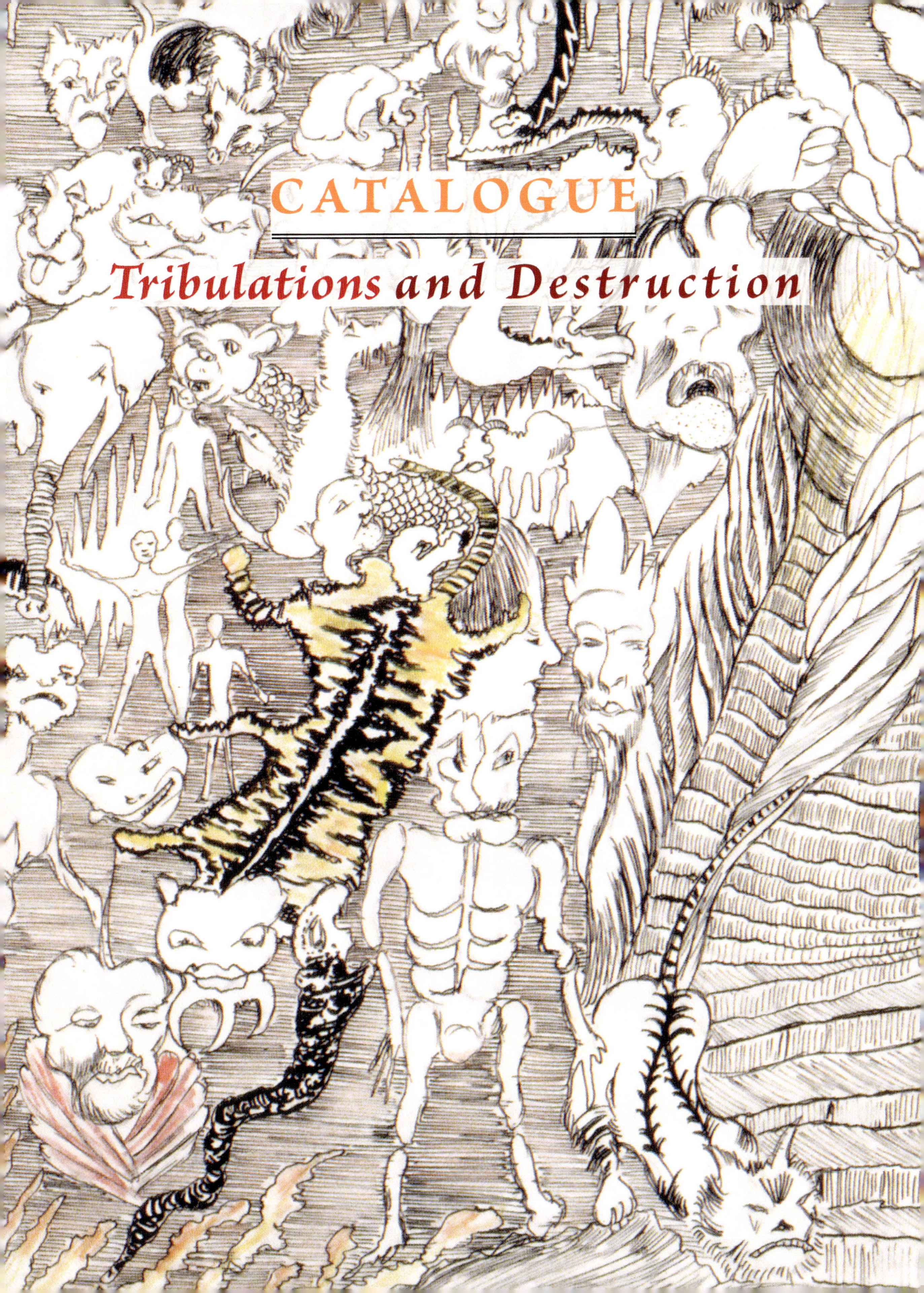

006 AFAI · Anonymous, untitled, undated.
Watercolor on paper, 20 x 14 cm
Picture Archive of the C.G. Jung Institute Zürich-Küsnacht
(This picture is discussed in Vicente de Moura's chapter.)

099 DUAA · Anonymous, untitled, 1964. Gouache on paper, 18 x 33 cm.
Picture Archive of the C.G. Jung Institute Zürich-Küsnacht

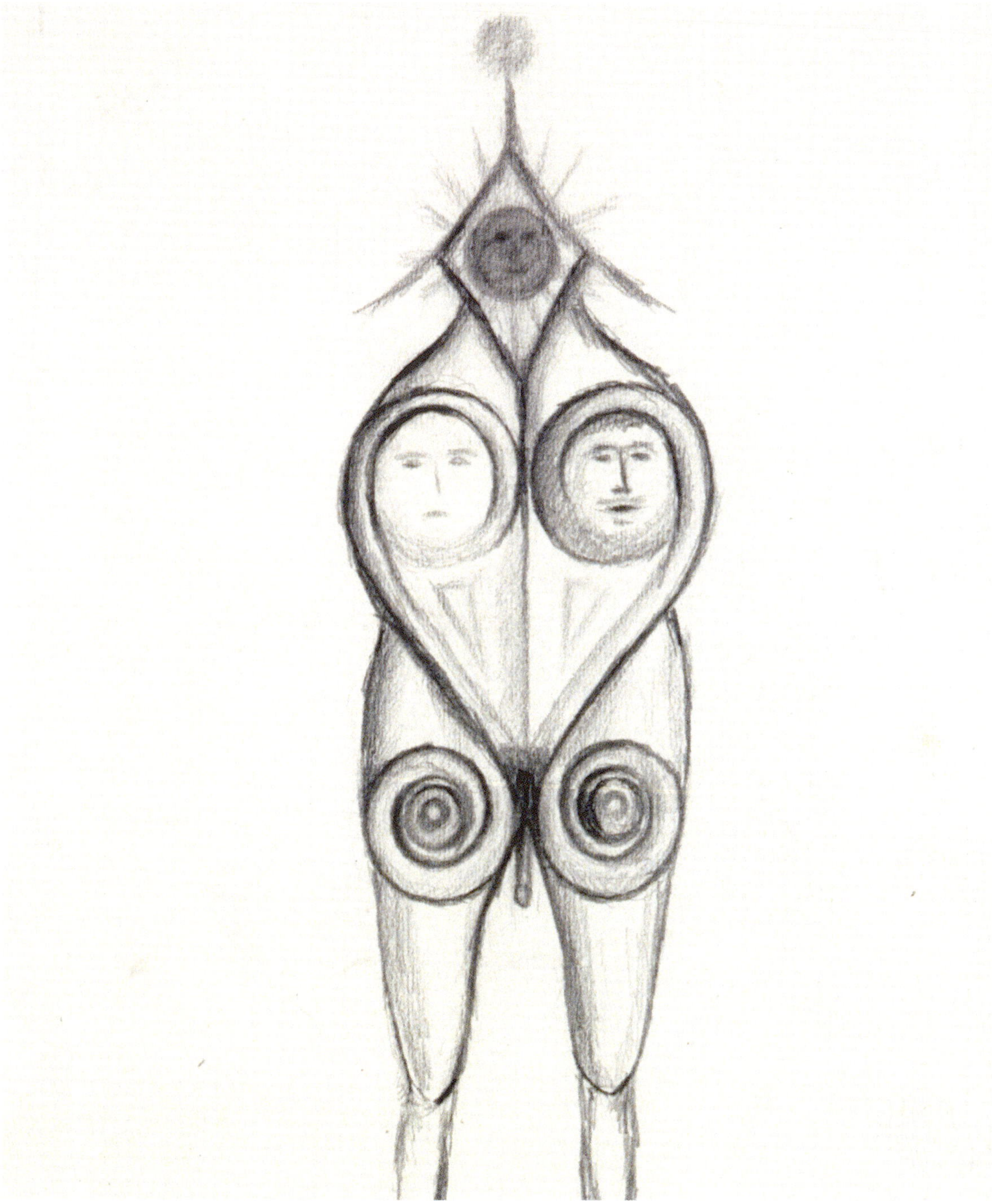

018 ARAE · Anonymous, untitled, December 1919
Pencil on paper, 21.5 x 28 cm
Picture Archive of the C.G. Jung Institute Zürich-Küsnacht

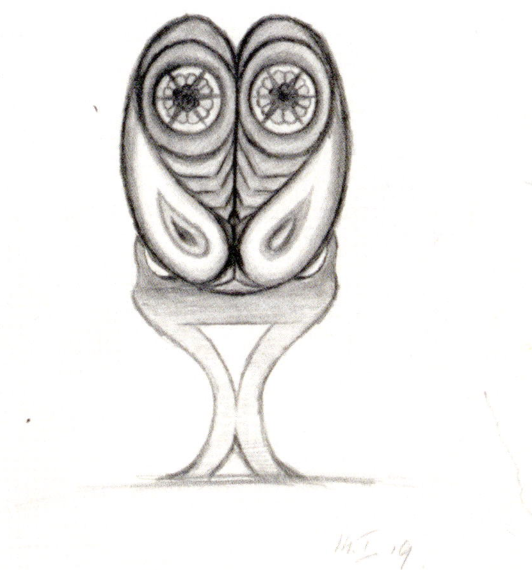

Upper: **018 ARAF** · Anonymous, untitled, 14 January 1919
Pencil on paper, 24 x 16 cm
Lower: **018 ARAX** · Anonymous, untitled, March 1919
Pencil on paper, 11 x 18 cm
Picture Archive of the C.G. Jung Institute Zürich-Küsnacht

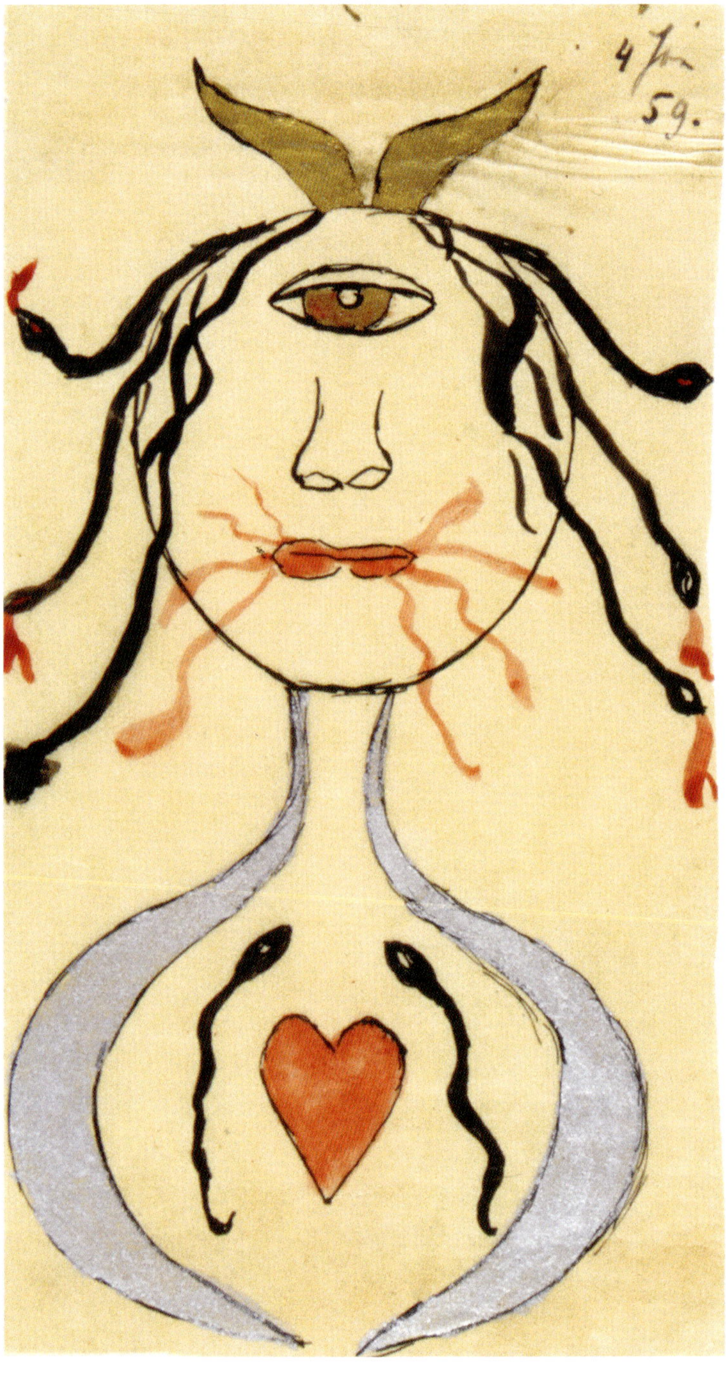

040 BNAT · Anonymous, untitled, 4 January 1959
Gouache and ink on paper, 16 x 9 cm,
Picture Archive of the C.G. Jung Institute Zürich-Küsnacht

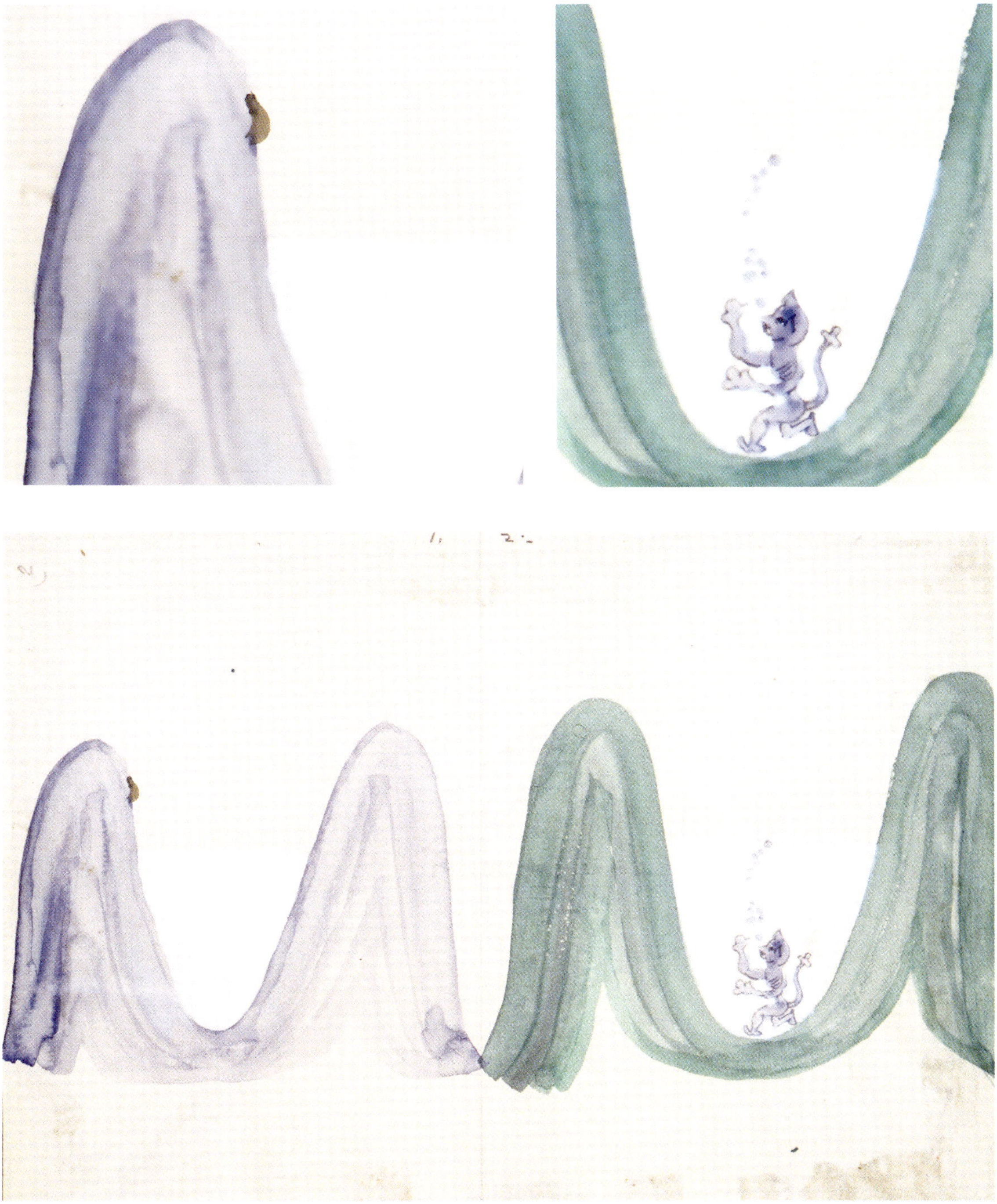

089 DKAB Anonymous, untitled, October 1945
Gouache on paper, 21 x 29 cm
Picture Archive of the C.G. Jung Institute Zürich-Küsnacht

023 AWAR · Anonymous, untitled, undated
Gouache on paper, 30 x 21 cm
Picture Archive of the C.G. Jung Institute Zürich-Küsnacht
Original to the right, enlargement below

083 DEAA Anonymous, untitled, undated
Gouache and ink on paper, 30.5 x 35.5 cm
Picture Archive of the C.G. Jung Institute Zurich, Küsnacht

026 AZAH · Anonymous, untitled, undated
Pencil on paper, 32.5 x 25.5 cm
Picture Archive of the C.G. Jung Institute Zurich, Küsnacht

023 AWAJ · Anonymous, "Rise and Fall", undated
Pencil and crayon on paper, 37.5 x 26 cm
Picture Archive of the C.G. Jung Institute Zurich, Küsnacht

034 BHAB · Anonymous, untitled, undated
Charcoal on paper, 48 x 34 cm
Picture Archive of the C.G. Jung Institute Zürich-Küsnacht

034 BHAC · Anonymous, untitled, undated
Charcoal on paper, 66 x 51 cm
Picture Archive of the C.G. Jung Institute Zürich-Küsnacht

034 BHAF · Anonymous, untitled, undated
Charcoal on paper, 51 x 66 cm
Picture Archive of the C.G. Jung Institute Zürich-Küsnacht

034 BHAI · Anonymous, untitled, undated
Charcoal on paper, 66 x 51 cm
Picture Archive of the C.G. Jung Institute Zurich, Küsnacht

034 BHAK · Anonymous, untitled, undated
Charcoal on paper, 66 x 51 cm
Picture Archive of the C.G. Jung Institute Zurich, Küsnacht

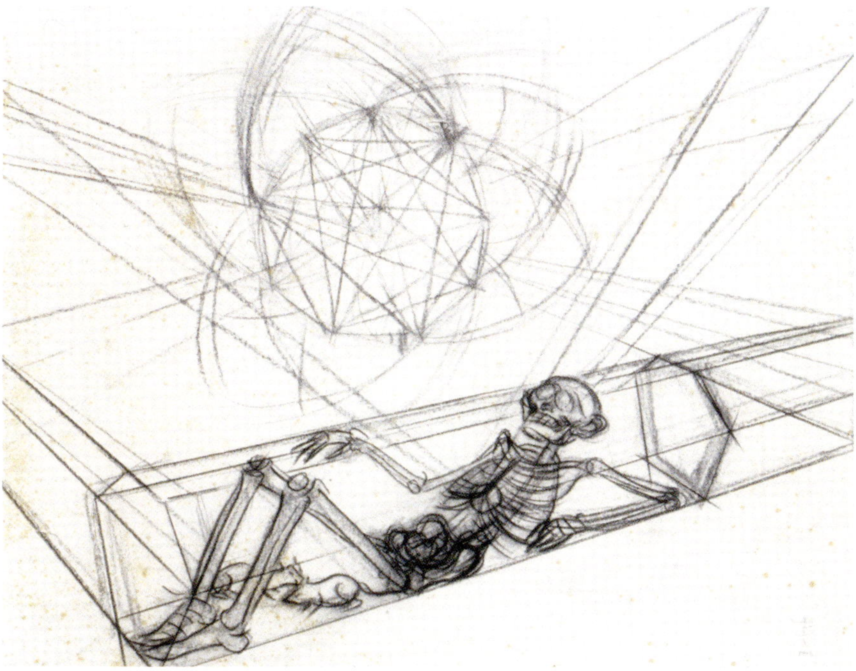

Top: **044 BRAC** · Anonymous, untitled, undated. Pencil on paper, 39.5 x 50 cm
Bottom: **044 BRAE** · Anonymous, untitled, undated. Pencil on paper, 31 x 41 cm
Picture Archive of the C.G. Jung Institute Zurich, Küsnacht

026 AZAE · Anonymous, untitled, undated
Gouache on paper, 25 x 19 cm
Picture Archive of the C.G. Jung Institute Zurich, Küsnacht

082 DDAB · Anonymous, untitled, undated
Ink on paper, 10 x 10.5 cm
Picture Archive of the C.G. Jung Institute Zürich-Küsnacht

050 BXAB · Anonymous, "Painting to represent myself", undated
Gouache on paper, 13 x 15.5 cm
Picture Archive of the C.G. Jung Institute Zürich-Küsnacht

072 CTAC · Anonymous, untitled, undated
Pencil on paper, 14 x 9 cm
Picture Archive of the C.G. Jung Institute Zürich-Küsnacht

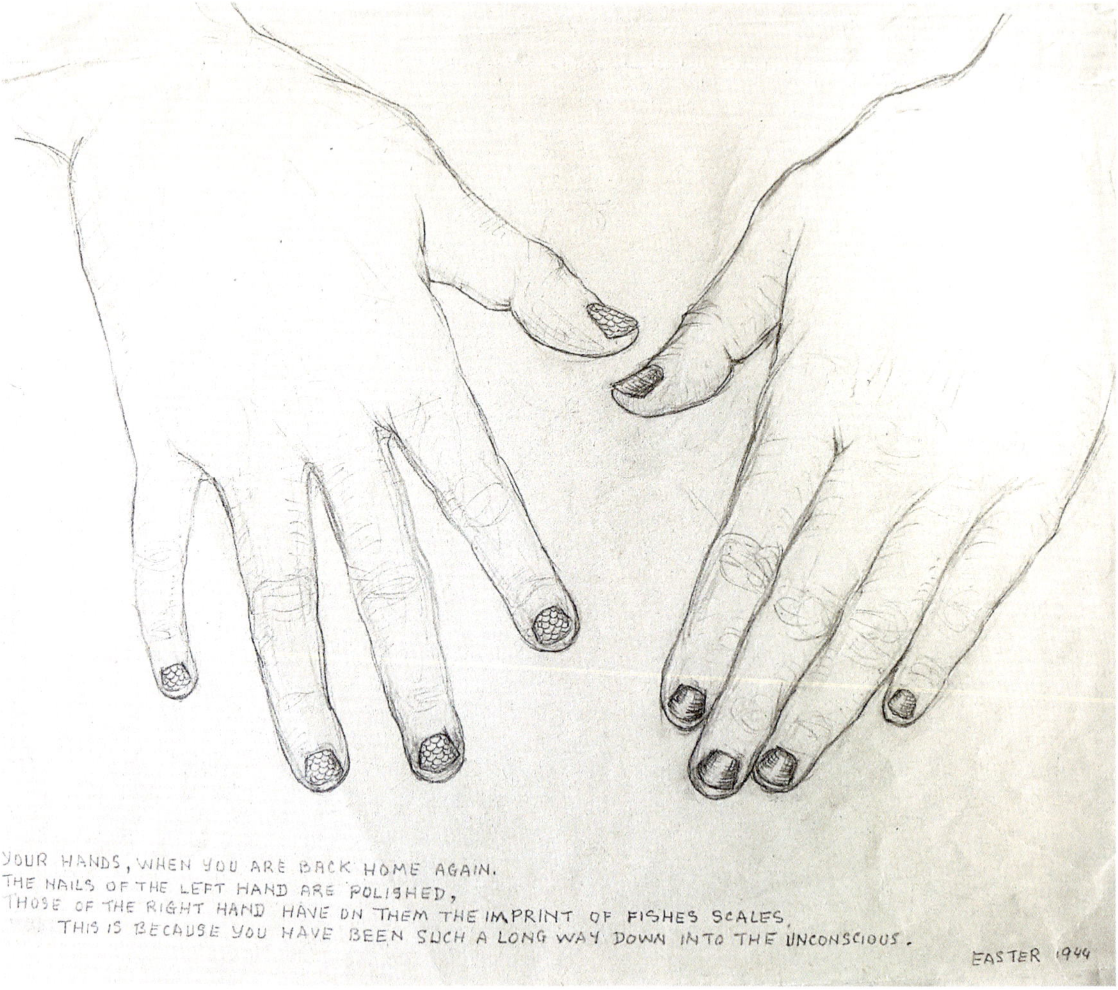

047 BUBS · Anonymous, "Your hands", Easter 1944
Pencil on paper, 25 x 29 cm
Picture Archive of the C.G. Jung Institute Zurich, Küsnacht

026 AZAH · Anonymous, untitled, undated
Pencil and watercolour on paper, 29.5 x 21 cm
Picture Archive of the C.G. Jung Institute Zürich-Küsnacht

Top: **012 ALAA** · Anonymous, untitled, undated. Pastel chalk on paper, 19.5 x 31 cm
Bottom: **012 ALAH** · Anonymous, untitled, undated. Pastel chalk on paper, 17.5 x 20 cm
Picture Archive of the C.G. Jung Institute Zürich-Küsnacht

069 CQAL · Anonymous, untitled, 16 January 1955. Ink on paper, 58.5 x 36.5 cm
Picture Archive of the C.G. Jung Institute Zürich-Küsnacht

The series of paintings on these two pages are discussed by Ingrid Riedel in her chapter, "Apocalyptic Times," with the exception of the painting in the lower left, **041 BOAD**.

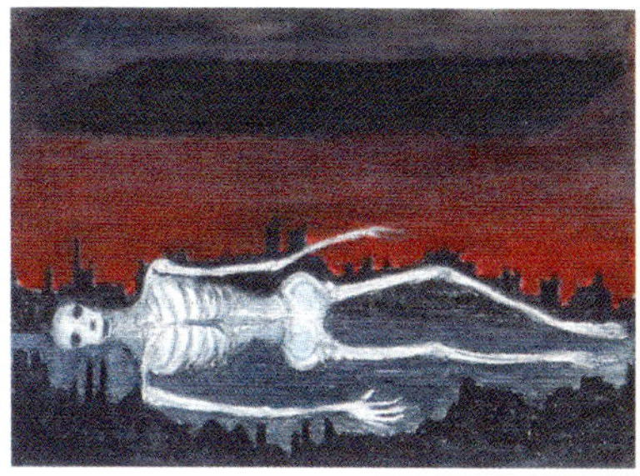

Picture Archive of the C.G. Jung Institute Zürich-Küsnacht

CATALOGUE:

Human and InHuman

015 AOAB · Anonymous, untitled, July 1926
Gouache on paper, 19 × 20.5 cm
Image Archive, C.G Jung Institute Zürich-Küsnacht

011 AKAA · Anonymous, untitled, undated
Gouache on paper, 24 × 18.5 cm
Image Archive, C.G Jung Institute Zürich-Küsnacht

014 ANAA · Anonymous, untitled, undated
Pastel on paper, 20 × 39.5 cm
Image Archive, C.G Jung Institute Zürich-Küsnacht

014 ANAB · Anonymous, untitled undated
Pastel on paper, 31 × 25 cm
Image Archive, C.G Jung Institute Zürich-Küsnacht

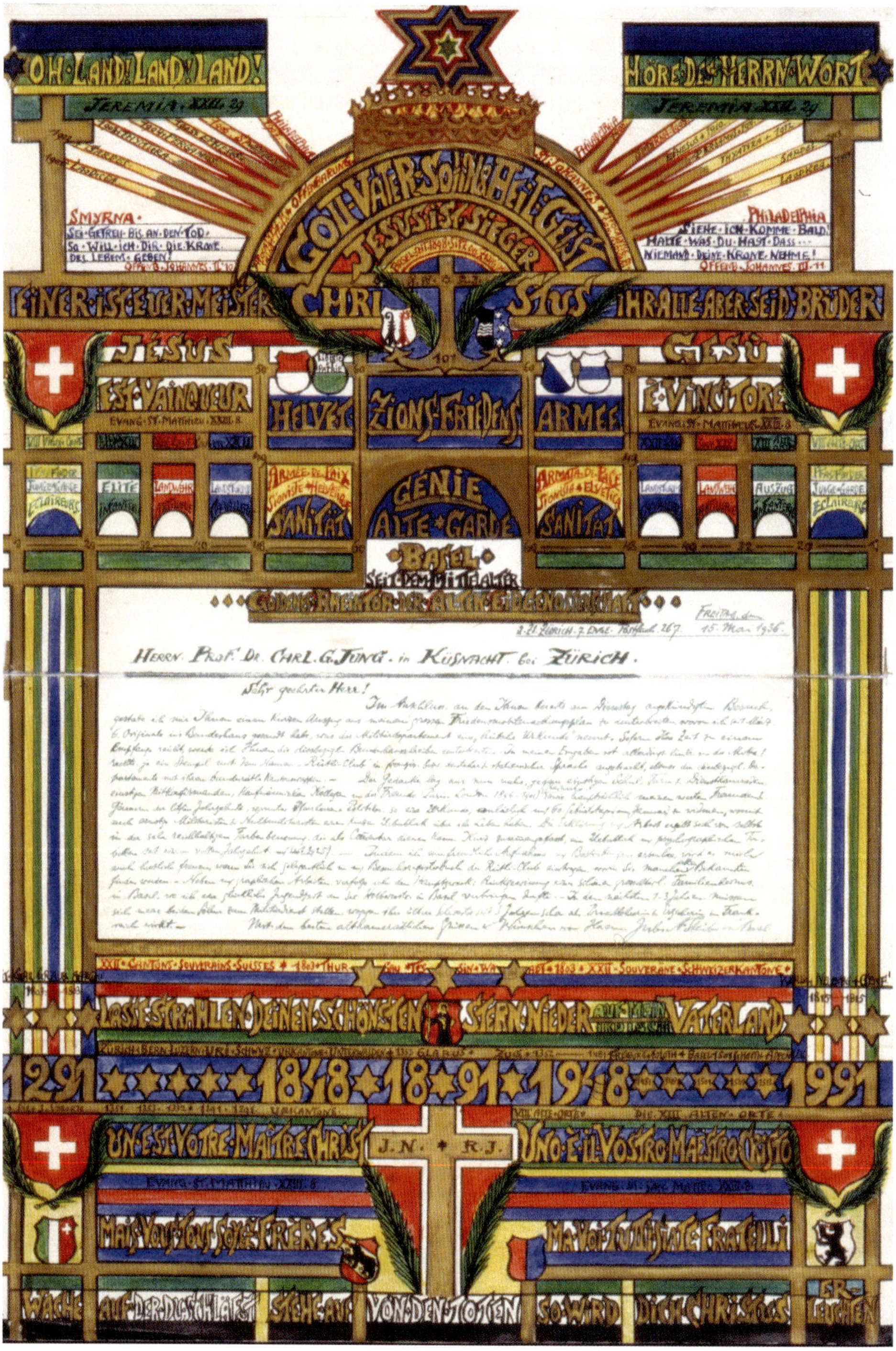

099 DUAN· Anonymous, "Oh, Land, Land, Land ...," 15. 5. 1936
Gouache and ink on paper, 45.5 × 31.5 cm
Image Archive, C.G Jung Institute Zürich-Küsnacht

095 DQEN · Anonymous, untitled, 19. 6. 1921
Gouache on paper, 32.5 × 25 cm
Image Archive, C.G Jung Institute Zürich-Küsnacht

095 DQOK · Anonymous, untitled, 1924
Gouache on paper, 25 × 35 cm
Image Archive, C.G Jung Institute Zürich-Küsnacht

095 DQOT · Anonymous, untitled, 18. 9. 1924
Gouache on paper, 32.5 × 25 cm
Image Archive, C.G Jung Institute Zürich-Küsnacht

008 AHAM · Anonymous, untitled, 24. 6. 1928
Gouache on paper, 28 × 22 cm
Image Archive, C.G Jung Institute Zürich-Küsnacht

Upper: 029 BCAA
Anonymous, untitled, 17. 1. 1924
Gouache on paper, 26 × 28 cm
Image Archive, C.G Jung Institute Zürich-Küsnacht

Lower: 029 BCAB·
Anonymous, untitled, 18. 1. 1924
Gouache on paper, 26 × 28 cm
Image Archive, C.G Jung Institute Zürich-Küsnacht

019 ASAI · Anonymous, untitled, undated
Gouache on paper, 43 × 32 cm
Image Archive, C.G Jung Institute Zürich-Küsnacht

025 AYAE · Anonymous, untitled, 11. 7. 1926
Gouache on paper, 14 × 14.5 cm
Image Archive, C.G Jung Institute Zürich-Küsnacht

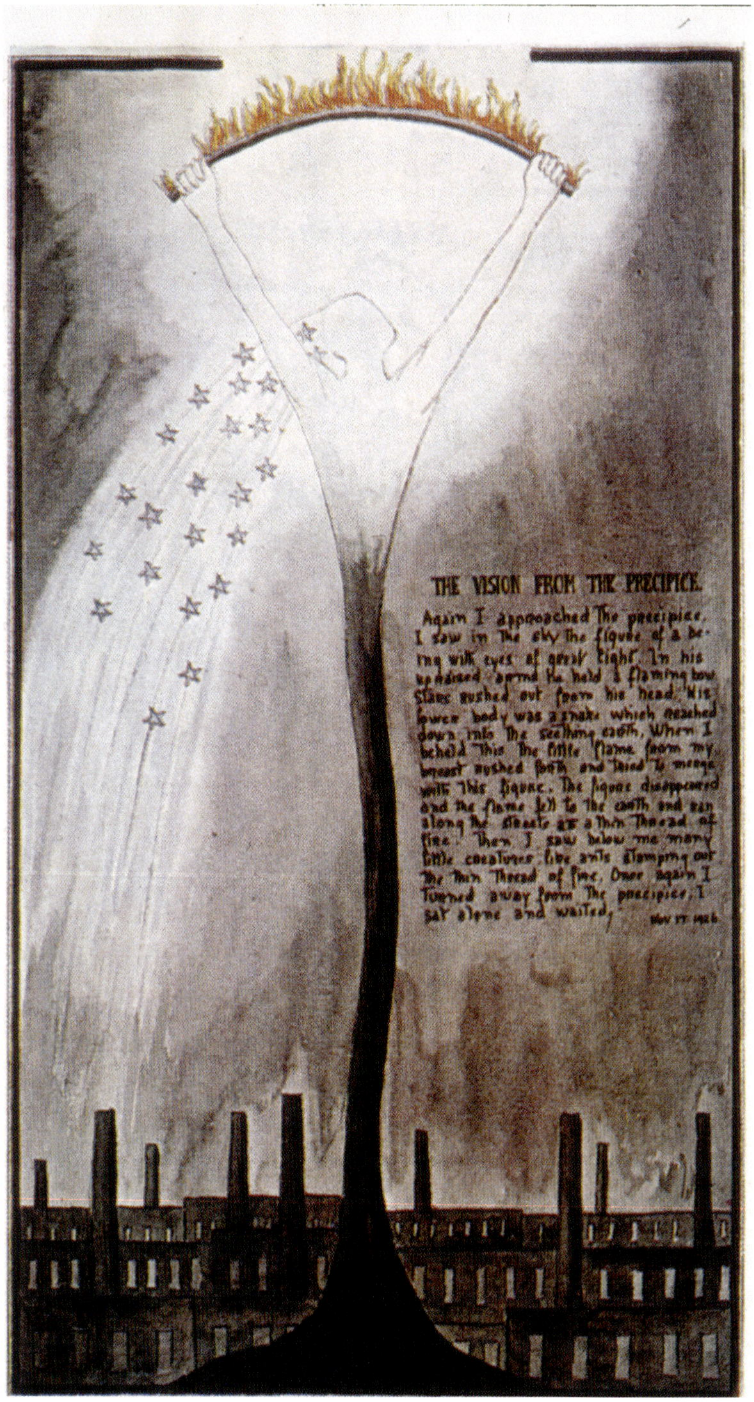

025 AYBR · Anonymous, "The vision from the precipice" ("Die Vision vom Abgrand"), 17. 11. 1926
Ink and gouache on paper, 22 × 14 cm
Image Archive, C.G Jung Institute Zürich-Küsnacht

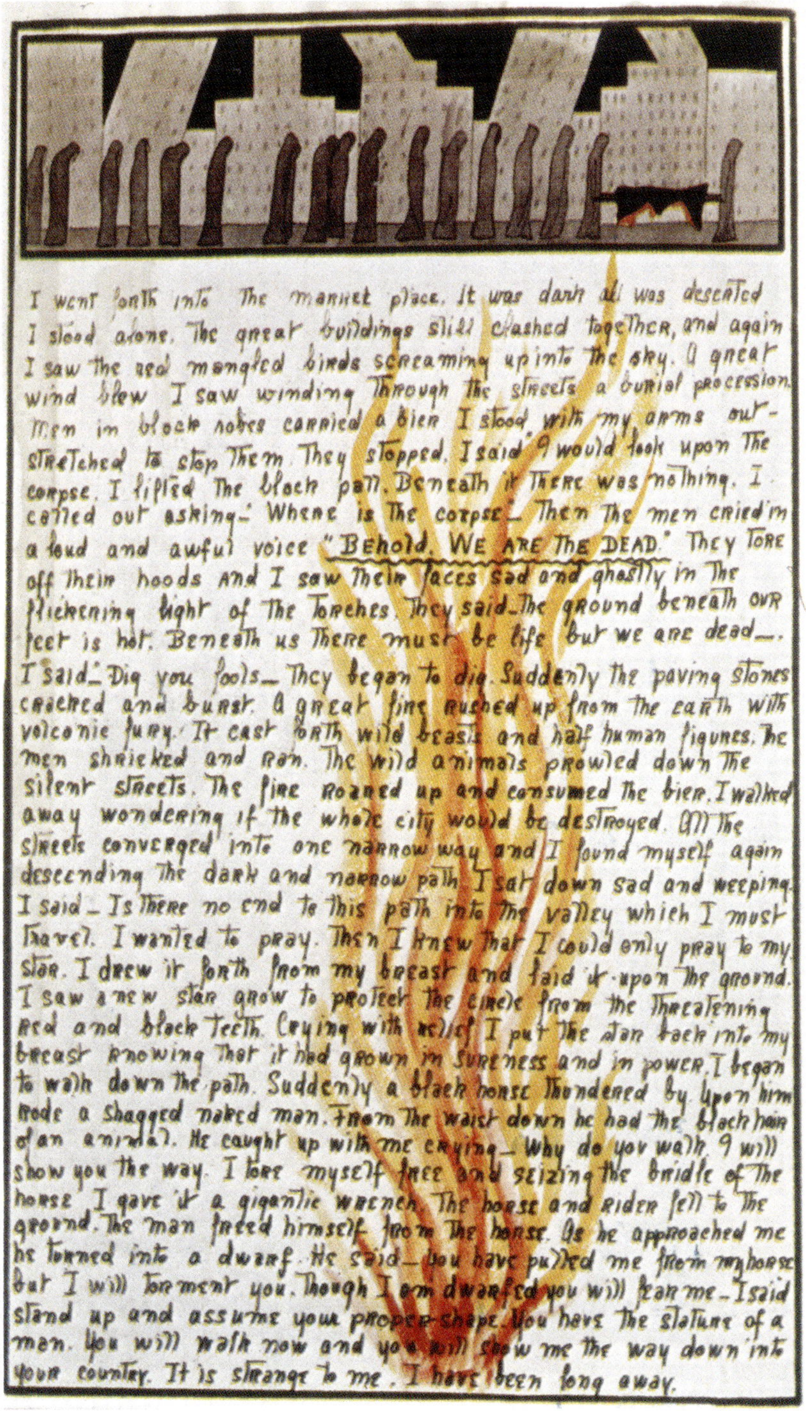

025 AYBU · Anonymous, "Behold. We are the dead" ("Siehe. Wir sind die Toten"), undated
Ink and gouache on paper, 18 × 14 cm
Image Archive, C.G Jung Institute Zürich-Küsnacht

043 BQAF · Anonymous, untitled, undated
Gouache on paper, 44.5 × 36 cm
Image Archive, C.G Jung Institute Zürich-Küsnacht

071 CSAB · Anonymous, untitled, undated
Pastel on paper, 31 × 21 cm
Image Archive, C.G Jung Institute Zürich-Küsnacht

105 EBNB · Anonymous, untitled, 1918
Colored pencil on paper, 23 × 30.5 cm
Image Archive, C.G. Jung Institute Zürich-Küsnacht

021 AUAF · Anonymous, untitled, undated
Gouache on paper, 21 × 30 cm
Image Archive, C.G Jung Institute Zürich-Küsnacht

076 CXFN · Anonymous, "Das Anhören der schwarzen Gedanken," 30. 9. 1940
Goache on paper, 29 × 21 cm
Image Archive, C.G Jung Institute Zürich-Küsnacht

026 AZAI · Anonymous, "Alles aus Liebe," undated
Gouache and ink on paper, 29.5 × 23 cm
Image Archive, C.G Jung Institute Zürich-Küsnacht

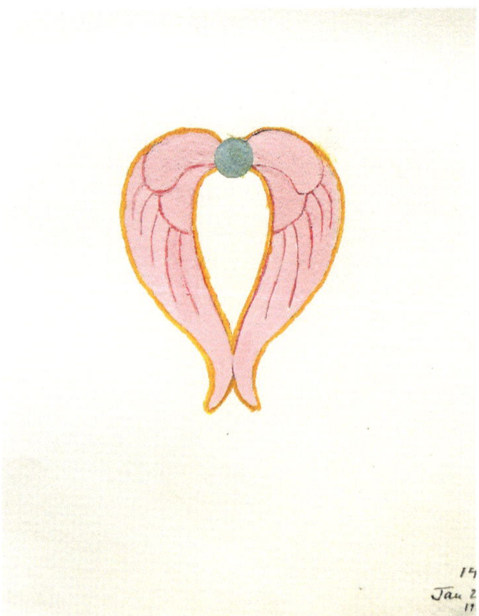

Upper left: 039 BMAL · Anonymous, untitled,
Text on reverse, 22. 1. 1928
Gouache on paper, 29 × 23 cm
Image Archive, C.G Jung Institute Zürich-Küsnacht

Upper right: 039 BMAM · Anonymous, untitled,
Text on reverse, 23. 1. 1928
Gouache on paper, 29 × 23 cm
Image Archive, C.G Jung Institute Zürich-Küsnacht

Lower left: 039 BMAN · Anonymous, untitled,
Text on reverse, 24. 1. 1928
Gouache on paper, 29 × 23 cm
Image Archive, C.G Jung Institute Zürich-Küsnacht

Lower right: 039 BMAO · Anonymous, untitled,
Text on reverse, 24. 1. 1928
Gouache on paper, 29 × 23 cm
Image Archive, C.G Jung Institute Zürich-Küsnacht

Upper left: **039 BMAP** · Anonymous, untitled,
Text on reverse, 25. 1. 1928
Gouache on paper, 29 × 23 cm
Image Archive, C.G Jung Institute Zürich-Küsnacht

Upper right: **039 BMAQ** · Anonymous, untitled.
Text on reverse, 27. 1. 1928
Gouache on paper, 29 × 23 cm
Image Archive, C.G Jung Institute Zürich-Küsnacht

Lower left: **039 BMAR** · Anonymous, untitled,
Text on reverse, 29. 1. 1928
Gouache on paper, 29 × 23 cm
Image Archive, C.G Jung Institute Zürich-Küsnacht

Lower right: **039 BMAS** · Anonymous, untitled,
Text on reverse, 30. 1. 1928
Gouache on paper, 29 × 23 cm
Image Archive, C.G Jung Institute Zürich-Küsnacht

039 BMBJ · Anonymous, untitled, 3. 3. 1928
Gouache on paper, 29 × 23 cm
Image Archive, C.G Jung Institute Zürich-Küsnacht

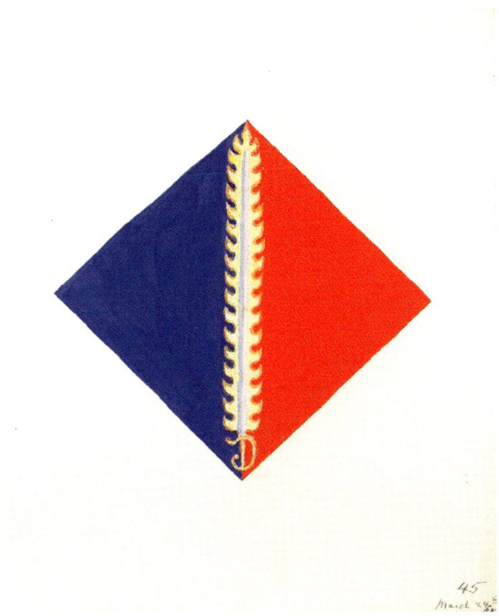

Upper left: **039 BMAT** · Anonymous, untitled,
Text on reverse, 2. 2. 1928
Gouache on paper, 29 × 23 cm
Image Archive, C.G Jung Institute Zürich-Küsnacht

Upper right: **039 BMAU** · Anonymous, untitled,
Text on reverse, 3. 2. 1928
Gouache on paper, 29 × 23 cm
Image Archive, C.G Jung Institute Zürich-Küsnacht

Lower left: **039 BMBU** · Anonymous, untitled,
Text on reverse, 24. 3. 1928
Gouache on paper, 29 × 23 cm
Image Archive, C.G Jung Institute Zürich-Küsnacht

Lower right: **039 BMCI** · Anonymous, untitled,
Text on reverse, 15. 6. 1928
Gouache on paper, 29 × 23 cm
Image Archive, C.G Jung Institute Zürich-Küsnacht

Upper left: **039 BMED** · Anonymous, untitled
Text on reverse, April 1929. Gouache on paper, 29 × 23 cm
Image Archive, C.G Jung Institute Zürich-Küsnacht

Upper right: **039 BMEK** · Anonymous, untitled,
Text on reverse, 16. 6. 1929.
Gouache on paper, 29 × 23 cm
Image Archive, C.G Jung Institute Zürich-Küsnacht

019 ASAF · Anonymous, "Blütenbaum" [Flowering Tree] about 1925
Embroidery on silk, 55 × 35 cm
Image Archive, C.G Jung Institute Zürich-Küsnacht

019 ASAA · Anonymous, "Vogel" ["Bird"], 1925
Embroidery on silk, 37 × 32 cm
Image Archive, C.G Jung Institute Zürich-Küsnacht

The Authors

Ruth Ammann, Curator of the Picture Archive at the C.G. Jung Institute in Zürich, trained architect, Jungian psychoanalyst, and sandplay therapist. Has worked in private practice since 1979. Training analyst and lecturer at the C.G. Jung Institute in Zürich. She served as President of the International Society of Sandplay Therapy for many years and has lectured all over the world.

Dr. Vincente L. de Moura, supervisor, instructor, and training analyst at the C.G. Jung Institute in Zürich. Former president of the Susan Bach Foundation. Has written numerous articles. From 1998 to 2015 Curator of the Picture Archive at the C.G. Jung Institute in Zürich. He is a trained psychologist, expert on Jungian typology for management consulting, and works as a psychotherapist in private practice.

Dr. Monika Jagfeld, art historian, Director of the Museum im Lagerhaus, Foundation for Swiss Naïve Art and Art Brut, in St. Gallen. She is a jury and board member of the EUWARD, European art award painting and graphic arts in the context of mental disability and board member of the European Outsider Art Association (EOA). Numerous exhibitions and publications on outsider art in historical institutional collections and the work of individual contemporary artists as well as involvement in crossover projects.

Dr. Verena Kast, professor of psychology and psychotherapist in private practice. Lecturer and training analyst at the C.G. Jung Institute in Zürich. She has written numerous highly acclaimed works on the psychology of emotions, foundations of psychotherapy, and the interpretation of fairy tales and dreams. Her most recent book in English: *Father-Daughter, Mother-Son. Freeing Ourselves from the Complexes that Bind Us*. Jungianeum, Asheville, N.C.: Chiron Publications, 2022.

Doris Lier, Lic.phil. (history, art history, general history of religion, and philosophy), Jungian psychoanalyst, lecturer, training and supervising analyst at the C.G. Jung Institute in Zürich and at ISAPZürich. Private practice since 1988. Various publications on history of symbols and dream interpretation as well as epistemological issues of analytical psychology. International lecturing activity.

Dr. Ingrid Riedel, Jungian analyst, theologian, and scholar of German language and literature. Honorary professor of the history of religion and psychotherapist in private practice in Konstanz, Germany and lecturer and training analyst at the C.G. Jung Institutes in Zürich and Stuttgart. Numerous books published by Patmos.

Dr. Philip Ursprung, art historian. Professor of the history of art and architecture at the ETH Zürich. He studied in Geneva, Vienna, and Berlin and has lectured at the University of Zürich, Universität der Künste Berlin, and Columbia University in New York. He is also editor of *Herzog & Meuron. Naturgeschichte* (Montreal, 2002) and author of *Die Kunst der Gegenwart* (Munich, 2010). His most recent book is *Der Wert der Oberfläche. Essays zu Architektur, Kunst und Ökonomie* (Zürich 2017). He is also Ruth Ammann's nephew and godchild.

CREDITS

All of the works from the Picture Archive of the C.G. Jung Institute in Zürich that are reproduced in this volume: © C.G. Jung Institut Zürich, Küsnacht.

Photos of the pictures: Ulrich Peters and Picture Archive of the C.G. Jung Institute Zürich, Küsnacht.

Chapter by Philip Ursprung
Fig. 1: Christ in a mandorla, central door of the west front, Chartres Cathedral: © akg-images / Catherine Bibollet
Fig. 2: Matthias Grünewald, "The Resurrection," Isenheimer altar: © akg-images.
Fig. 3: Giovanni Battista Piranesis, "Caceri III (The Round Tower)": © akg-images.